## REVISED EDITION

# TIMING the MARKET

### How to Profit in **Bull** and **Bear** Markets with Technical Analysis

## Curtis M. Arnold

**IRWIN**
*Professional Publishing®*
Chicago • London • Singapore

# Table of Contents

# PREFACE

Whether you're interested in stocks or commodities, whether you believe that prices are going up or down, it has been proven time and time again that the most reliable method for timing the markets is technical analysis.

The problem is that most investors think it's best left to professionals—people who are willing to wade through a room full of charts and graphs . . . consult all sorts of esoteric, quasi-mystical indicators . . . and maybe throw a dart at the board on the sly. *Nothing could be further from the truth!*

Technical analysis is simply a method for forecasting market trends and timing critical turns—for generating specific buy or sell signals based on readily obtainable information. It's accurate, unemotional and *very profitable*. Moreover, now, for the first time, it's well within your grasp. You should read this book if:

- You have an interest in making every dollar you invest produce maximum profits, with minimal risk.
- You invest in any market, anywhere in the world, including stocks, bonds, futures, precious metals, real estate, rare coins or tangibles; puts and calls, mutual funds, money funds and more.

- You're either an active or a passive investor.
- You're a seasoned professional or an absolute beginner.
- You want to control your investments, rather than your investments (or someone else) controlling you.
- You realize that others, no smarter than you, are making fortunes utilizing the modern principles of technical analysis.

This book has much to offer you, today, tomorrow, and long into the future. Starting with the history of the very first individuals who recognized the value of unemotional, empirical analysis of market data . . . and continuing through the entire current spectrum of techniques, market indicators, their profitable application, and their underlying principles . . . you'll be guided along the road that leads to real comprehension of technical analysis.

You'll learn virtually effortlessly, about charts and graphs, everything about a myriad of technical indicators, how to construct your own technical system and, most importantly, how to profitably interpret the results.

Technical analysis is not merely a set of rules and formulas that you learn once and then put into practice. It represents the collective experiences of thousands of traders who made, and often lost, huge sums of money over the years.

# PROLOGUE:

# THE SECRETS OF THE PAST

Imagine that we are back in the early part of this century. Much like today, market volatility is tremendous, trading volume is on the rise, and, as in today's futures markets, small losers are everywhere; but large winners are few and far between.

Who are they? Where can we find them? As we shall soon see, they are a small handful of traders who were flying in the face of conventional wisdom, ignoring the strict fundamental principles of their time, and developing their own unique technically based theories and trading systems.

We walk into the second-floor offices of a small, smoked-filled brokerage firm. The floor is littered with debris of thousands of trades and streams of ticker tape. We discover that the real technical analyst is not the "customer's man" behind his desk or the senior partners in the back offices. Rather he is the 14-year old boy scurrying to post the numbers on the quotation board while another clerk, sitting by the ticker, calls out the prices. His name: Jesse Livermore.

Having a good memory for figures, he begins to detect certain patterns in the behavior of stock prices before they embark on an advance or decline. We follow him through adulthood, and we see that, by perfecting his tape-reading into a science, and by putting up only 10 percent margin, he is able to multiply his capital many times—so much so that he is eventually trading huge blocks of stock. This gives him the ability to "test" the market before he commits himself heavily.

You ask: "I don't get it, Jesse. How do you do it?"

"Here's how it works: If I want to buy a stock, I will first start selling into the market. If the price doesn't go down, I conclude that there's good support for that stock at that level, that it's safe to buy. Conversely, if the stock's price does go down easily, I'll continue selling it, driving the price down still further until it can find support."

"But how can you tell?"

"From the volume, from the price action, from the rhythm of the ticker. You can *feel* when you're touching bottom."

This is both fascinating and disappointing. You know that in today's massive markets, you will never be able to "test the markets" like Livermore did. They're simply too big. But you make a mental note to yourself that when you get into this book on technical analysis you will pay close attention to the many techniques that use his basic principles. You will seek to quantify them in a way that you can readily comprehend and profitably utilize . . . even if you're not blessed with intuitive genius.

Our next stop is the home of a man by the name of W.D. Gann. As he opens the door to invite us in, we are struck by the obvious contrast in his style and approach. Livermore was a hands-on practitioner who learned his techniques during market hours. This man is a tireless student who pours over his charts into the wee hours of the morning.

"What stocks do you own right now, Mr. Gann?"

"Stocks? Own?" comes the puzzled response. "None!"

You later discover that he is about to complete 10 years of research on over 100 years of stock market fluctuations—both in the U.S. and in England—before making his first investment. His homework certainly pays off. Legend had it that he eventually amasses over $50 million from his speculations in stocks and commodities.

"The basis of market movements," he asserts, "can be found in natural laws. You may think I'm crazy, but this is why I have spent so many years studying astrology, numerology, and the great pyramids. Here, look at this! See these diagrams? They show the common link that is all-pervasive—the importance of time, cycles, and seasonality."

"Yes, but, how can you use that to make money in the stock market?"

He smiles. "Gentlemen, stocks, like atoms, are the centers of energies which are controlled *mathematically*. In other words, the Law of Vibration can help to accurately determine the exact points to which stocks or commodities should rise and fall within a certain time frame. Learn those laws of nature. Plot their time and space coordinates on your charts. And more often than not, you will be able to predict the future with amazing accuracy."

You're not convinced. You wonder if this is more mysticism than science. So you spend days and months pouring over his actual forecasts. You are shocked to discover that the forecasts are too accurate to be attributed to sheer luck or coincidence. Later, however, when you return to the 1990s and try to apply his knowledge to today's markets you will find that no one is able to duplicate his incredible results. You will be occasionally frustrated by the flagrant ambiguities that permeate his work, and you may begin to wonder that perhaps Gann never did reveal—to us or to anyone else—his ultimate discoveries.

You are heartened, however, by one fact: Even though his successes cannot be duplicated, others have taken great inspiration from Gann's work and gone on to develop valuable technical tools of their own. Like them, you are inspired by his belief that nothing is too farfetched or to insignificant to bear investigation and further research . . . regardless of how often others ridicule your novel notions.

For now, however, you're anxious to get down to some really straightforward analysis. So we take you to a man by the name of Richard D. Wyckoff. At first, he reminds us a bit of Jesse Livermore; he's a consummate tape-reader.

"The future course of prices," he tells us, "can be determined by a careful analysis of volume which, when combined with the skills of tape-reading, gives you a solid three-dimensional picture of the market. The key to your success will be to seek out—and then act upon—the *patterns of accumulation and distribution. Do not act unless you are prepared.*"

"In what sense?" we inquire.

"Anyone who buys or sells a stock, a bond or a commodity for profit is speculating if he employs intelligent foresight. If he does not, he is gambling. But never place blind faith in any one system. Stock market technique is not, and never will be, an exact science. Stock prices are made by the minds of men. Whatever technical analysis you do, remember that you—not your technique—are the boss . . . with discipline and without emotion, of course. Breaking your own rules is like cheating at solitaire. But, no matter how good your technique, you will still need a healthy dose of human judgment for your final decision."

"OK. But what *is* your technique? Tell us exactly how you go about picking a bottom."

He leans back in his chair as you prepare yourself for a detailed explanation. "Here. Let me run through it step by step: Remember, you must watch out for accumulation. Look for a period of several months of lateral movement at the bottom of a downwave. That's when large traders are gradually buying in the face of negative sentiment and selling to the public." Wyckoff pauses.

"Is that it?" you ask.

"No. In fact, I believe I have actually identified six distinct price/volume behavior patterns which occur during the accumulation process. First, there's what I call 'preliminary support' on a day when you see a marked increase in volume and a temporary halt to the decline. Second, you'll usually get a resumption in the downtrend and what I call a 'selling climax' on extremely heavy volume. But watch out for one *minor* detail of *major* importance: Toward the end of that day, prices bound up to close significantly above the lows of the day. Third, you can start looking for an *automatic* rally which results from short-covering. Fourth, prices eventually *retest the low of* the selling climax on lighter volume. This is your *secondary test.* A trading range follows which may last several months. Eventually, prices rally strongly off the lows of the trading range on heavy volume. This is your first real *sign of strength*. The next correction has very narrow daily ranges. It's the *last point of support* and your last chance to get in before the new uptrend begins. Finally, once an uptrend has been completed, you will probably see a similar but inverted pattern near the top—during *distribution.*"

You lean over and whisper. "Aha! Now we have something concrete, something we can sink our teeth into. Let's start rolling with real money!"

Wait a minute! This is just one example of the many concepts contributed by technical analysts reviewed in this book. Besides, before we return to our time, we have one last stop to make in the 1930s—to talk to a gentleman by the name of R. N. Elliott.

"They say I'm a revolutionary or some kind of crackpot, but some day I think people will find my theory quite rational. [In fact, it later will be known as Elliott Wave Theory.] Here's what I've discovered: Specific patterns in price movement are caused by swings in mass investor psychology—from pessimism to optimism and back again. I have identified 13 distinct patterns into which all stock market movements can be classified."

"You mean time and cycles like in Gann's work?" we ask.

"Not exactly. I place more credence in the *formations* that prices exhibit on charts. The stock market—indeed, any market—unfolds according to a basic rhythm or pattern of *five waves up* and *three waves down*. The three waves down are a correction of the preceding five waves up. But that's not all. There is a precise proportionate relationship—in time and magnitude—between the distances traveled during each of the waves. I call it the *Golden Ratio*. Some people are vaguely aware of these waves and call them "thrusts" or simply "moves." But they don't know how to count them; they can't seem to tell where one ends and the other begins; and most important, they don't realize that the waves are often related to one another by the Golden Ratio of .618—a ratio which, by the way, is also found in the growth of snails, the logarithmic expansion of the universe and the Great Pyramids."

When you return to the present time, you wonder out loud: "What good has it done us to discover the techniques that worked fifty years ago? Aren't markets totally different today?"

To which we respond: "Yes, on the surface, they are, and our ability to track and quantify them is certainly superior. But the basic forces that drove prices up and down in previous generations are still at work today. All markets—both then and now—are simply auctions; and all auctions, no matter what the technology, are governed by the same general principles of supply and demand. The price of a stock or commodity today, as in the past, mirrors investors' expectations of the future—their collective emotions of hope, fear, and greed. It is the ability of technical analysis to identify and predict these future perceptions of value that makes it such a valuable tool."

If you want to be a writer, you read Shakespeare, Dickens, and Twain. Likewise, if you want to do technical analysis, you must study Livermore, Gann, Wyckoff, Elliott, Dow, and others. This is not just because they are "the classics," but also because most modern-day technical analysts have incorporated many of their trading techniques. In this chapter, we have seen only a capsulized glimpse into their market theories. It's by no means enough to do justice to their great works. But we hope it will whet your appetite to explore their ideas more fully. In any case, subsequent chapters of this book review many of today's major technical indicators, most of which have their "roots" firmly planted in the past of these pioneers.

# PART I

## HOW TO PROFIT
## FROM TECHNICAL ANALYSIS

# 1

# TWO ROADS TO SUCCESS IN THE MARKETS

---
---

The time is the first half of the 1990s. Stretched out before you are the widest diversity of markets, with the most powerful leverage and the greatest opportunities—*or dangers*—in all economic history. You are both bewildered and fascinated by the speed of change and the plethora of technical indicators used to track that change.

However, before you can move into this new, often uncharted territory, you come to a series of crossroads, where you must make some basic decisions regarding how you will approach the markets in general.

At the first crossroad you are confronted by a stranger who asks you: "Do you want to be a *picker* or a *follower*?"

"What do you mean?"

"The pickers are all those that try to pick a bottom or pick a top. They say that they have technical tools which will predict the next market turn, help them get in before it really makes its move and get out just before it heads back in the other direction. For lack of a better term, we call them *'bottom-pickers'* and *'top-pickers.'* But more often than not, they're the ones who, in effect, get picked off . . . like flies."

"Every time there's the slightest rally or correction, you can hear them shouting 'this is it! Now's the time to buy (or sell).' Granted, there are some who do make money, but for the most part they suffer from what we call the ICGAL syndrome—that die-hard belief that "It Can't Go Any Lower."

The stranger points toward the horizon. "See over yonder. That's where you'll find the ceremonial burial ground of the thousands of would-be traders who literally got killed trying to pick "the bottom" in copper, lumber, sugar, gold, crude oil and virtually every commodity imaginable. Some of them actually had a better-than-normal batting average. But they bounced in and out of the markets so often, their equity got eaten alive by commissions, even discount commissions.

"The *followers* use a somewhat more conservative approach. Rather than trying to catch the entire move, from top to bottom, their brand of technical analysis is geared to giving them *confirmation* that the market is indeed trending in one direction or another. Then, and only then, do they jump on board. So they're the *trend-followers*."

"So what's so bad about that?"

"Nothing at all. Trouble is, more often than not, by the time they get in, the market has *already* moved substantially and is ripe for a correction, a sudden reversal in the opposite direction. Often the followers stick it out for a while until their losses are unbearable. Then they bail out just before the market is ready to move their way again. In the final analysis, what many wind up doing is exactly the opposite of what they should be doing; they buy near the top and sell near the bottom! You can find *their* burial ground adjacent to that of the *pickers*.

You're discouraged. Is this what it's all about? Losing money left and right, getting decimated by choppy, unpredictable markets where nothing works? For many, the answer is yes. It's not for lack of technical tools, though. It's because they commit one or more of the cardinal errors of investing.

## THREE FATAL ERRORS

**Error #1. They overtrade.** They're too anxious to always *do* something and they do it with too many shares or contracts. Several years from now, if you remember nothing else from this book, do remember this: Trade consistently in *modest* amounts so you can always stay cool and unemotional about any particular trade.

**Error #2. They are overly influenced by what they hear or see outside of their own technical work.** Even the most seasoned professionals can fall prey to this malady. It's only natural; humans are social animals. But to be successful, you must act independently, as a loner. If you listen to someone else, he may get you in at the right time, but will he be there to tell you when to get out?

We believe you should either make *all* of the decisions or you should make *none* of the decisions by employing a money manager with a good track record. If you bought this book, we assumed you have chosen the former, at least for a portion of your funds.

**Error #3. They don't have a simple set of procedures, or if they do, they don't follow them.** The indicators in this book are the building blocks for you to build your system—trading rules that you can follow without ambiguity. Once you have such a system, try it out on paper for a few months. Then take token amounts. And finally, if it works to your satisfaction, shift into full gear. But do not arbitrarily, because of fear, greed or any other reason, break your own rules. By trading modestly, you can afford to stick with your system until it either proves itself or bombs out. If you change course midstream, however, you will never know for sure.

## THE SPIDER STRATEGY

The fact is that, although there are many small losers in the markets, there are also a small number of very large winners! You *can* pick tops and bottoms. But to do so successfully, you must follow what we call **the spider strategy.** The spider does not need to "feed" every day. He is content to wait until a morsel comes his way, patient and secure in the knowledge that he has taken the steps necessary for his survival.

His carefully crafted web transmits to him all sorts of information. But he knows how to identify the false signals—the wind vibrating his web, a drop of rain—from the real thing enmeshed in it. Why does he know it so intimately? Because he has carefully constructed his web himself. No one else can build it for him. As a result, the configuration of his web is as uniquely his as his finger prints. Most important, the spider is patient. He waits until he sees a *convergence* of most or all of his indicators before he acts; but when he does, he pounces aggressively and without hesitation.

If you follow this strategy, you will use, among others, those indicators which tell you when a market is "overbought" and vulnerable to a decline, or conversely when it is "oversold" and ripe for a move up. These are the so-called "oscillators"—the indicators that oscillate back and forth, like an electrocardiogram, from the top and the bottom of a predefined range.

One of the most common of these is **momentum** which measures and plots the net change from one period to the next. Imagine the pendulum on a grandfather clock, swinging from one extreme to another with a momentum that carries it as far as it can go in one direction . . . before reversing to the other direction. The same is true for markets.

## THE OMNIPRESENT APPROACH

You can also make money trend-following. Here however you must employ what we call the *omnipresent* approach. In other words, you have to maintain small positions in many different markets at all times. You must be willing to go short (more on short selling later) any market that is trending down and buy any market that's trending up, not hesitating to reverse your positions when the market reverses. You will absolutely need—at all times—a diversified portfolio. (Stocks alone cannot give you enough diversification, no matter how many different industries you're in!) Your portfolio should have at least one position in each major market sector—not only stocks, but also precious metals, bonds, foreign currencies, agricultural commodities, etc.

Most important, in order to win with trend-following, you must be willing to accept a large number of relatively small losses in order to stay on board for a small number of very large gains. During choppy sideways periods, you must have enough money in the kitty to withstand a steady erosion in your equity. And during big moves, you need the courage to stay with your position until your trend-following system tells you to get out, no matter how anxious you may be to grab a profit. In this book you will find several methods for trend-following, among which moving averages are probably the most common and easy to use.

Remember, although helter-skelter trend-following is indeed hazardous, with a systematic and disciplined approach you will indeed make money using this approach. There will be ups and there will be downs. But as long as you steer clear of the three cardinal errors, you should wind up with substantial profits in most years.

*Before you get too deeply into technical analysis you will come to one more crossroad. You see a signpost just ahead with a question in bold letters . . .*

# 2

# TO COMPUTE OR NOT TO COMPUTE

While that decision is both personal and economic, please allow me to make one major point: a computer is nothing but a fast pencil; and neither will make you a penny in the markets if you don't use them!

Let there be no doubt. All of the great pioneers of technical analysis did their work completely without the benefit of a computer. For example:

Charles Dow. He died in 1902, so we think we can safely rule out any possibility that he used computers. The great Russian economist/cycle analyst Kondratieff . . . who perished in a prison camp somewhere in Mongolia. I seriously doubt that they furnished him with a personal computer!

Perhaps one of the best current examples would be Joe Granville . . . he got his great inspiration for his "On Balance Volume" theory while sitting in the bathroom of a major brokerage firm in New York in the early 60s. An electric hand-dryer? Maybe. But we assure you there wasn't a computer in sight! On the other hand there are many who might say that the computer has done for technical analysis what the Gutenberg printing press did for the printed word.

Have you ever asked yourself questions such as these: In the last 10 years, if you had bought silver on each new moon and sold it on the full moon, would you have made money? In the last two years,

9

if you bought the S&P 500 Index at each Thursday's close and sold it at each Monday's open, what would the results have been? Technical analysts of the past rarely asked these types of questions—not so much because they appear to be irrelevant—but primarily because they didn't have the time, energy and, frankly, the means, to find the answers. Today, the speed of the computer makes answering "what if" questions like these a breeze. It's simply a matter of historical testing or "simulation."

What do *I* think about all this? Very simple: Technical analysis can be performed *with* or *without* a computer. What computers have accomplished is primarily to help you with the "grunt work"—to eliminate much of the drudgery with mathematical calculations required to apply some of today's more popular analytical techniques.

A personal computer will allow you to track a far broader range of indicators in a much larger universe of markets, increasing many times the number of good choices available to you. In addition, there are certain kinds of analysis that require so many calculations, doing them by hand would be very difficult. For these reasons I recommend that you seriously consider using a personal computer to expand your technical analysis horizons.

# WHY TECHNICAL ANALYSIS WORKS

There are several schools of thought. One school believes in the theory behind **chart formations and patterns.** They read charts much like ancient astrologers read the stars, looking for "head and shoulders" formations; "Ms" or "Ws"; or "wedges," "flags" and "pennants." These, they believe, reflect the patterns of buying and selling, accumulation and distribution, or market psychology.

Others have demonstrated that these formations are merely the sum total of various **cycles.** Edward R. Dewey, perhaps the preeminent cycle researcher and analyst of this or any other century, defined them as "the tendency of events to repeat themselves at more or less uniform intervals . . . the pulsations of distant stars . . . the prevalence of sunspots . . . weather conditions . . . the abundance of mammals, birds, insects and fish, and the prices of securities."

The big problem however is this: Which cycle is now impacting the market? The temperature reading at 12 noon on February 8th is determined by a convergence of cycles of different length—the 24-hour cycle of the earth rotating on its own axis, the 12-month cycle of the rotation around the sun, and longer-term weather cycles which may be as long as five years or more, and so forth. The same goes for markets, except it's not always so clear which cycle is now in force.

Finally, some of the most successful traders are those that use **market sentiment.** The theory is that if too many people are **bullish** (optimistic) about the market going up, the market is ripe for a decline as they take profits or are forced to get out. Conversely, if too many are **bearish** (pessimistic), it implies an up move may be in the making.

R. Earl Hadady's organization, publishers of *Bullish Consensus (Market Vane)*, is in the forefront of this type of research. A wide range of investment advisors and analysts are polled every week for their views on virtually every market. These data are then compiled with a formula which factors in (a) how strongly the advisor feels about each market and (b) how many followers he or she has.

## INTERNAL MARKET COMPOSITION

Whether you're talking about stocks, bonds, precious metals, foreign currencies or commodities, there is one fact which is virtually immutable: If it's held by **strong hands,** the likelihood of a sudden bout of selling is greatly reduced. Any news, whether normally interpreted as "good" or "bad," will tend to trigger a rise. If it's held by **weak hands**, the most likely move will be down.

In this book we present various methods for timing the markets. However, my personal view is this: *The key to timing the markets is accurately tracking the strong hands vs. the weak hands—what they own and when, in what relative proportions and, perhaps most important, how this critical "market composition" is changing from one month to the next.*

But, who are the strong players? And who are the weak ones? How do we keep track of them accurately and on a timely basis? In the stock market, the strong hands are the insiders; and the weak hands are the odd-lot buyers.

In future markets, the strong hands are the **commercials** or **hedgers,** those who buy and sell futures almost exclusively as a protection against price changes in the actual bonds, stocks, currencies or commodities which they own. The weak hands are the **speculators,** especially the **small speculators** who are in the market strictly to make a quick profit and are not involved in the business of producing, selling or buying the actual bonds, stocks or commodities.

Certainly there are some speculators who do extremely well in the markets, making substantial profits year after year. And, conversely, there are no doubt some commercials who often perform poorly. But when taken as a group, there can be absolutely no doubt about one thing: The commercials are usually the **winners** and the speculators are usually the losers. How do you know when a major move is about to begin? Very simple: You just look for a significant **imbalance** between them—*a visible departure from the normal trading pattern.*

A typical example is what happened to the price of oil in 1985. Throughout the summer, the press was full of news about the great world oil glut. Sheik Yamani of Saudi Arabia threatened to take "drastic action" to boost production.

But behind the scenes, where very few were looking, an important shift was taking place. Hoards of small speculators were going short crude oil, heating oil and other oil products. Meanwhile, a few big oil companies, with vast capital reserve to back them up, were buying heavily on a scale down. Soon oil prices began to move higher, and continued to march upward for most of the remainder of the year.

By the end of November, after prices had risen steadily for nearly five months, these positions had been reversed. Now it was the little guy who owned the oil and the big guy who was on the other side of the market. Sure enough, as soon as OPEC abandoned its pricing policy, there began one of the sharpest price declines in recent history. It proved that the small speculator had been right in the first place. Trouble is, his timing was lousy, and he failed to stick to his guns.

In the futures markets, the data which shows the positions held by small speculators, large speculators, and commercials is released by the Commodity Futures Trading Commission in Washington, D.C. The report, known as the Commitment of Traders report is now issued biweekly. This data is also carried by newswires and by some chart services. While this information is critical in making informed decisions in the futures markets, the raw data is not very informative unless it is viewed in a historical light. Therefore, in the mid-1980s I created an index (C.O.T. Index) which creates useful information from the raw data.

The C.O.T. Indexes rank each market as bullish or bearish on a scale of 0-100 percent. The ranking is devised by comparing the commercials' net long or net short positions to historical levels. For example, if the C.O.T. Index registered 100 percent in copper, we would know that commercials were net long (or less net short) than at any time during the past four years. A reading like this would typically occur in a downtrend that had been in progress for some time and would put us on the alert to cover our shorts and look to buy. A second index I devised is called the Movement Index. It gauges the change in the previous reading of the C.O.T. Index. When a large change occurs in the Movement Index, it signals that commercials have recently made significant commitments in the market and could be acting on inside information. My indexes are published in the *Bullish Review*, 14600 Blaine Avenue East, Rosemount, MN 55068.

# PART II

## THE BASICS OF TECHNICAL ANALYSIS

# 4

# TECHNICAL ANALYSIS AND CHARTING

There are essentially two methods of investing or speculating in markets. You can use external or "fundamental" information such as the profit outlook of an individual company, overall economic forecasts or the potential supply and demand of a particular commodity.

Or you can use strictly internal or "technical" information which ignores the fundamentals and focuses instead upon the actual patterns in the price movements and the actual buying and selling in the marketplace. The advantages of the technical analysis are very clear:

1. Unless you have a very sophisticated and accurate forecasting model (even the largest computer models in the world—at Brookings Institute, Chase Econometrics or the Federal Reserve Board—are notorious for their inaccuracies) or unless you subscribe to the newsletter of a very astute forecaster, by the time you receive the information, most other investors have also received it and have reacted accordingly, pushing the price up or down. In other words, the fundamental information is almost invariably *already* reflected in the market.

17

2. There are so many contradictory fundamentals impacting the market at any one time and so many "structural changes" in how these fundamental factors interact that it is often impossible to know how to weigh them. Again, this process of evaluation is all done by the marketplace itself and reflected in the price.

3. In addition, your computer can readily zero in on technical analysis and make cold and unbiased judgments; whereas fundamental information would normally require much more extensive interpretation on your part.

When you stop and think about this, it will become clear. You can't possibly know more about the value of a company's stock than its own board of directors. Likewise, in the commodity markets, you will never know more about crop conditions or the supply and demand factors at work on a certain commodity than the actual professionals that work in that industry. Fortunately, however, you don't have to.

Hundreds of years of price charts have shown us one basic truth—*prices move in trends.* A trend indicates there exists an inequality between the forces of supply and demand. Such changes in the forces of supply and demand are usually readily identifiable by the action of the market itself as displayed in the prices. Certain patterns or formations which appear on the charts have a meaning and can be interpreted in terms of probable future trend development.

Charts are the working tools of the technical analyst. Until very recently, most charting was done manually. At best, you could subscribe to a chartmaking service (of which there are many excellent ones). They produce daily charts which are mailed to you weekly. You then put in the prices each day until your new chartbook arrives the following week—no problem as long as you are not trying to follow too many stocks and commodities. If you are, however, it could be quite a time consuming job. This is where a computer *would* come in handy.

If you own a computer, you have a further advantage in charting—flexibility. When you are dependent upon a chart service, you must see the market from the perspective which they arbitrarily select. Your computer, on the other hand, allows you to control the amount of history you wish to view. You may change the spacing between days. You may look at the data as daily, weekly or monthly. You have the ability to magnify selected portions of the chart. The following examples—representing the same general period for the Dow Jones Industrial Average—show how identical price patterns may be viewed through different perspectives using the graphical capabilities of your computer.

Figure 4-1 is a simple high-low chart packed tightly with *no* space between each day's price.

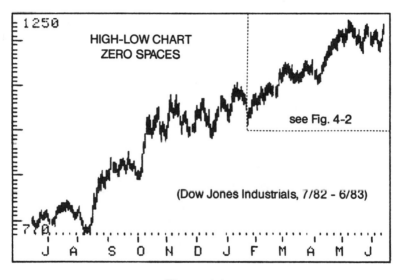

HIGH-LOW CHART
ZERO SPACES

see Fig. 4-2

(Dow Jones Industrials, 7/82 - 6/83)

J  A  S  O  N  D  J  F  M  A  M  J

**Figure 4-1**

But notice in Figure 4-2 how the pattern is clarified by adding one space between each day's price, although now only half of the time span fits on the page.

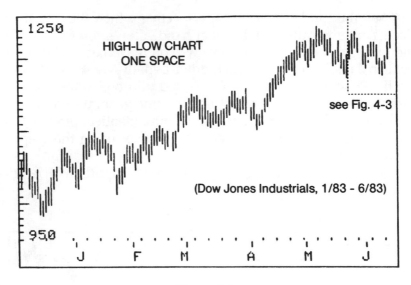

**Figure 4-2**

Figure 4-3 provides an entirely different perspective as nine spaces are added between each day's price.

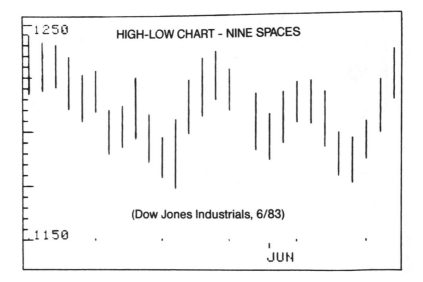

**Figure 4-3**

Figure 4-4 adds two additional elements of information—the opening and closing price for each day.

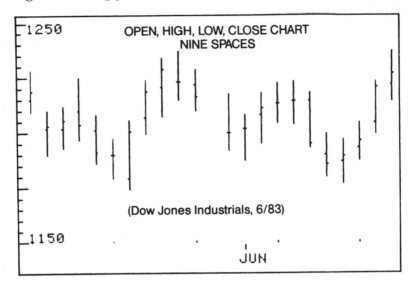

Figure 4-4

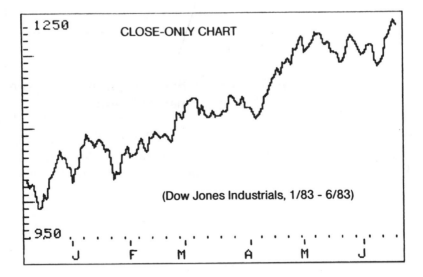

Figure 4-5

Figure 4-5 is a "close only" chart—one continuous line connecting each day's close. It is an extremely valuable analytical tool rarely offered by chart services.

In Figure 4-6, we adjust our scales so as to make the price pattern appear flatter, still another advantage of your computerized charting.

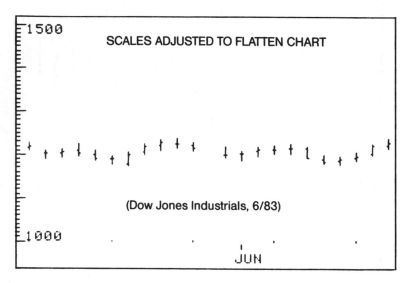

**Figure 4-6**

You can view a much broader time perspective in Figure 4-7 which uses data in weekly—rather than daily—form.

These are only a few of the myriad possibilities. The charts themselves, however, are not the goal. Rather, they are simply a handy device for revealing to you—at a glance—critical trends and chart patterns which will help guide your investment decisions.

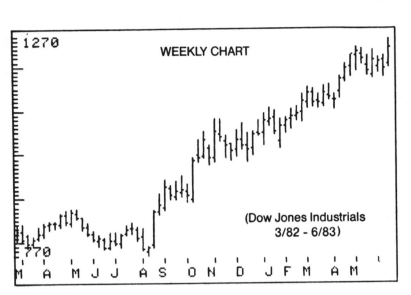

Figure 4-7

# TRENDS AND TRENDLINES

Prices move in trends because of an imbalance between supply and demand. When the supply of a stock or commodity is greater than the demand, the trend will be down as there are more sellers than buyers; when demand exceeds supply, the trend will be up as buyers "bid up" the price; and if the forces of supply and demand are nearly equal, the market will move sideways in what is called a "trading range." Eventually, new information will enter the market and the market will begin to trend again either up or down, depending on whether the new information is taken as positive or negative.

Remember, you can still profit in **both** and *uptrend* or a *downtrend* by *buying* or *selling short*—selling borrowed stocks which you hope to buy back later at a lower price. When you buy, it is said you are "going long" and you "are long" or "stay long" until you sell out. When you sell short, the expressions used are "go short," "be short" or "stay short." A major uptrend is a "bull market" and an opportunity to profit by being "bullish." A major downtrend is a "bear market" so you will want to stay "bearish." The key to trend analysis, of course, is to determine *when the pattern will change* so that you can shift in time from bearish to bullish or vice-versa.

Trends which are very brief are called *minor* trends; those lasting a few weeks are known as *intermediate* trends; and trends lasting for a period of months are *major* trends.

**TRENDLINES** will help you determine what trend is in force. If a market is moving up, you draw a line connecting each successively higher bottom. As long as the market remains on or above this line, the uptrend is in force. Conversely, in a downtrend, you would draw a line connecting each successively lower top. As long as prices remain on or below this line, the downtrend is in force.

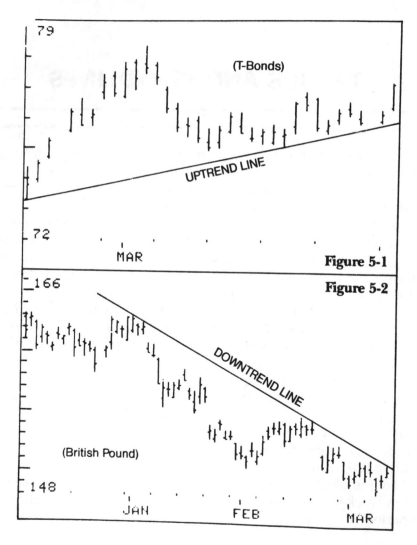

Figure 5-1

Figure 5-2

Trendline theory states that once a trendline is penetrated, the trend which was previously in force is reversed. Thus, if an uptrend line is penetrated, it is a signal to sell; and if a downtrend line is penetrated, it is a signal to buy. But there is still more to know about trendlines.

Let's say your downtrend line has just been decisively broken and you now believe we are starting a new uptrend. You can't draw a new uptrend line yet because you only have one bottom. You must wait until prices move higher for about a week, then react downward for a couple of days, and later start moving higher again. This will give you a second, somewhat higher bottom which you can connect to the first bottom to form an uptrend line. So far, so good.

If prices, after moving higher, react downward and form a third bottom on the trendline, the trendline then becomes more valid. We say that prices "tested" the trendline and it "held." The longer this trendline remains intact, the more authority it will have.

You will find that very steep trendlines are not very authoritative in that they will often be broken by a brief sideways movement or "consolidation," after which prices shoot up again. It is the trendlines with the gentler slope—either upward or downward—that usually offer more technical significance.

In sum, factors to consider in weighing the validity of a trendline include: (a) number of bottoms (or tops) that have formed on or near the trendline, (b) the overall duration of the trendline and (c) the steepness of the angle.

Getting back to our example, what if the market accelerates and a third bottom is formed way above our trendline? Now where is the real trend?

We may have to wait until the fourth bottom forms before we know for sure. Until then, it would be a good idea to draw in two trendlines, A and B.

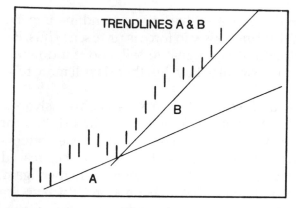

**Figure 5-3**

**FAN LINES.** When a market drops sharply, you will of course have a steep downtrend line. Often this trendline will be broken by a sharp rally, at which point a new trendline must be drawn. At a later date, this second trendline might be broken by a rally and a third trendline would need to be drawn. Such lines are known as "fan lines."

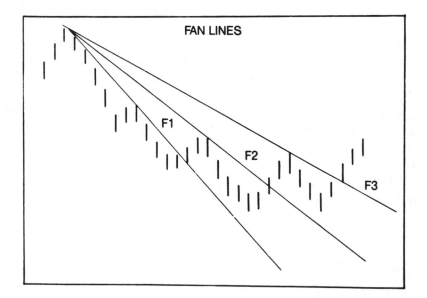

**Figure 5-4**

The rule is that when the third fan line has been broken, the trend has changed to the upside. In rising markets, this rule can also be applied in reverse.

**VALID PENETRATIONS.** As stated earlier, a penetration of an uptrend line is a signal to sell; and a penetration of a downtrend line is a signal to buy. But let's not forget that charting is an art and not a science. Therefore, we must appraise the validity of the penetration. Here are a few questions to ask when a penetration occurs:

Was penetration by just a small amount? If so, it remains suspect and we must look at other factors.

Did the price actually *close* below the trendline or was it merely the low of the day which broke the trend, an event which we call penetration on an "intraday basis"? An intraday break often is not sufficient evidence to confirm a change in trend; and even the close itself should be *significantly* below the trendline.

Did *volume* pick up on the day in question? If so, there is a good chance the trendline break was valid. Was the break accompanied by a gap or a reversal pattern? (Gaps and reversal patterns are discussed in Chapters 7 and 9.) If so, this would also lend credence to a change in trend.

Conversely, did the penetration occur as a result of several days of sideways movement? This would look more like a test of the trendline than a penetration of it. Further movement up or down should be awaited before a conclusion is drawn.

**"PULLBACKS"** or "throwbacks" are very interesting phenomena that often occur after the breaking of a trendline. Here's what happens in this case: An uptrend line is broken. Prices continue lower for a few days. Then they rally back right up to the trendline again. Finally, the market proceeds to move lower. (The reverse would occur upon the breaking of a downtrend line).

In the example illustrated in Figure 5-5, you can see that the pullback actually caused prices to go higher than the price at which the trendline was broken. Thus, had you sold short when the trendline was broken, you would have a loss a few days later. One way many professionals handle this situation is to wait for the pullback

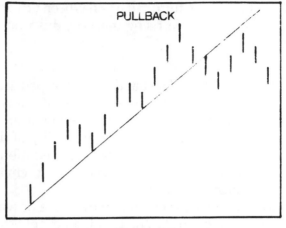

**Figure 5-5**

before selling short. One problem here it that sometimes the pullback never materializes and you wind up selling short at much lower levels or missing the move completely. I usually recommend selling half of your positions on the trendline break and the other half on the pullback.

**TREND CHANNELS**. In an uptrend, you can construct a trend channel by drawing a line *parallel* to the uptrend line using as your starting point an intermediate top made between two successively higher bottoms.

**RETURN LINE.** This second line is often called the "return line" since it marks the area where reaction against the prevailing trend originates. The area between the basic trendline and the return line is the "trend channel."

This return line is less reliable than the basic trendline but is valuable enough to be considered in your trading strategy. One short-term trading strategy applied by professionals in an up market is to buy on or near the basic trendline and take profits on or near the return line. Another variation on this technique is to draw a parallel line equidistant between the basic trendline and return line.

Now you have an upper channel or "sell zone," and a lower channel or "buy zone" (Figure 5-7).

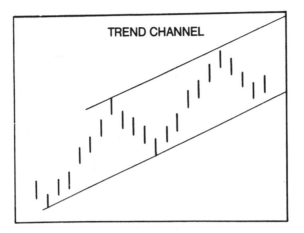

**Figure 5-6**

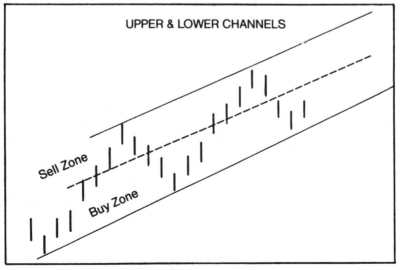

**Figure 5-7**

A return line can also be used to forewarn of an impending change in trend. Any time prices fail to move up to the area of the return line, you can consider the market is weakening. Use this as a warning and be on the alert for a break of the trendline the next time prices approach it.

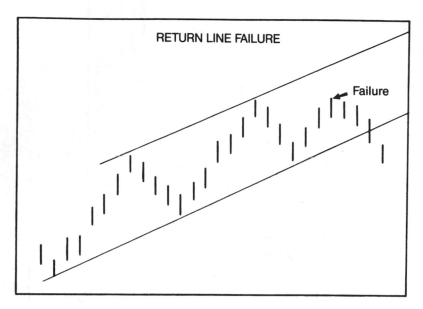

**Figure 5-8**

The main problem with trendline analysis is that it's too easy and, as a result, many an investor and trader can follow it, pushing prices up or down prematurely, making it difficult for you to make *your* trade in time to catch the move. Therefore, in Chapter 7, we delve deeper into chart analysis to find ways of *predicting* a break in a trend—*before* it becomes obvious to the average investor. But first let's examine one more critical factor—volume.

# 6

# VOLUME

In the stock market, volume refers to the number of shares that change hands on a given day. In commodity markets, it refers to the number of contracts traded. Each transaction is the result of the meeting of demand, on the one hand, with supply on the other. When demand exceeds supply, prices tend to rise. Conversely, when supply exceeds demand, prices tend to fall. Therefore, volume occurring during advances is termed "demand volume"; volume occurring during declines is "supply volume."

We study volume because it can be a measure of supply and demand. There are many ways to visualize the relationship of volume and prices. Some analysts think of volume as a gauge of market pressure. My own particular "picture" is this: Imagine you have turned on the garden hose and are pointing it skyward. You toss a plastic ball into the stream of water, and it shoots upward. But if you turn down the water pressure, what happens to the ball? It continues upward from its own momentum for a second or two, but then falls back. It can't continue higher until you increase the water pressure. Like the plastic ball, prices need increasing volume to continue higher. When prices move higher, but on diminished volume, they are likely to fall back.

The basic rules of volume analysis are as follows:

1.   When prices are rising and volume is increasing, the present trend will continue, i.e., prices will continue to rise.

2.   When prices are rising and volume is decreasing, the present trend is not likely to continue, i.e., the price rise will decelerate and then turn downward.

3.   When prices are falling and volume is increasing, the present trend will continue, i.e., prices will continue to fall.

4.   When prices are falling and volume is decreasing, the present trend is not likely to continue, i.e., the price decline will decelerate and then prices will turn upward.

5.   When volume is not rising or falling, the effect on price is neutral.

How can technical analysis employ this concept in practical applications? Let's assume XYZ stock has been in a trading range for several weeks with an average daily volume of 50,000 shares changing hands. Prices now begin to move higher and the daily volume picks up to 80,000 shares. We are justified in believing that prices will continue higher, fueled by "demand volume." Sure enough, prices do continue to move higher on strong volume over the next three weeks.

Then, in the fourth week, prices tumble and lose 30 percent of their previous gains. Do we sell the stock or hold? Again, the clue lies in the volume picture. We notice that during the fallback, XYZ stock has been trading only 40,000 shares per day. Therefore using our volume rules, we can surmise that this is only a *temporary* reaction. What might be actually happening in the marketplace? Any number of factors could be contributing to the fall in prices. Early buyers could be taking profits or any new buyers could be waiting for a setback before buying. All of these are natural, healthy reasons for a correction and, therefore, we have no reason to abandon our position at this point . . . unless we notice that volume is beginning to increase on down days.

As expected, in week 5, prices begin shooting up again on volume averaging 90,000 shares a day. Week 6 continues in the same way. Week 7 brings a reaction in prices, but again on reduced volume of 50,000 shares per day. We hold our stock. Week 8 sees prices rising again to new highs, but volume—oddly enough—is only averaging 60,000 shares per day. This is a clear-cut warning signal: Demand volume is drying up. New demand may still come into the market if favorable news events occur, but if not, prices are in danger. Remember, prices can only go up if fueled by rising demand volume, but if they fail to get that extra boost, they can fall under their own weight. As expected, prices turn down the next few days on heavy volume; we sell our stock.

The XYZ example represents only one possible scenario. What if prices have been in a sideways trading range and then begin to fall on low volume. Would we consider this move false? Not necessarily. Although prices must be accompanied by strong volume to confirm an up move, *down* moves often begin on light volume. Remember, a market can fall under its own weight; and it is important to be aware that *volume usually tends to be lighter when prices are falling than when rising*.

In the XYZ example, the last phase or "leg" of the move was on light volume. But oddly enough, tops may also be formed on *heavy* volume—a "climax" which usually occurs after a market has been moving up for a considerable amount of time.

This is a contradiction which reflects a classical problem which has puzzled technical analysts for many years and there is no complete solution. However, if you closely observe the market action it may help you determine if it is a climax or not. Typically, prices make new highs in the morning on heavy volume, but by afternoon, prices are substantially lower while volume is still heavy, producing a reversal day (see Chapter 7). This is a classic example of "distribution"—a period when previous owners of the stock are dumping their shares and taking profits, while Johnny-Come-Latelies are buying it at the top. The previous owners who have been buying for weeks have more stock to distribute than the Latelies can handle. So, supply overcomes demand, prices crash, and the new buyers are left holding the bag. Stocks are said to be "moving from strong hands to weak hands."

Bottoms often display quite the opposite pattern, occurring on

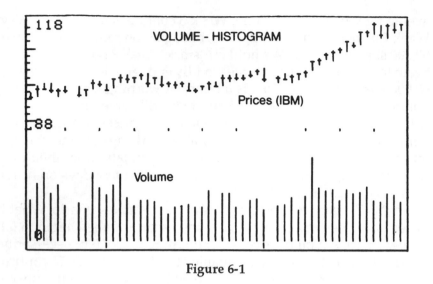

Figure 6-1

light volume. Volume tends to dry up, indicating a lessening of supply pressure. If prices then move higher on increased volume, it is a good sign that the decline has ended.

How do we graphically represent volume? The traditional way has been in the form of a bar chart directly beneath the price chart (Figure 6-1).

However, you need not be so limited. You can also look at volume in many different ways. When looking at the actual volume itself, I prefer to chart it as a continuous line, rather than as a bar chart. Notice also, I have more space between each day's price so I can readily identify the corresponding change in volume for *each* day (Figure 6-2).

Some analysts feel that the absolute change in volume from day to day is not as important as the deviation from the current average volume. Again, by using your computer as an analytical tool, you can be way ahead of those who must rely only on commercially produced charts. Here's what you do: First, run a 10-day moving average on volume (for more on moving averages, see Chapter 13). Then run a continuous line of current volume on the same graph. If the current volume line is above the 10-day moving average, we know that the volume is increasing. Conversely, when the current volume is below the 10-day moving average, volume is decreasing.

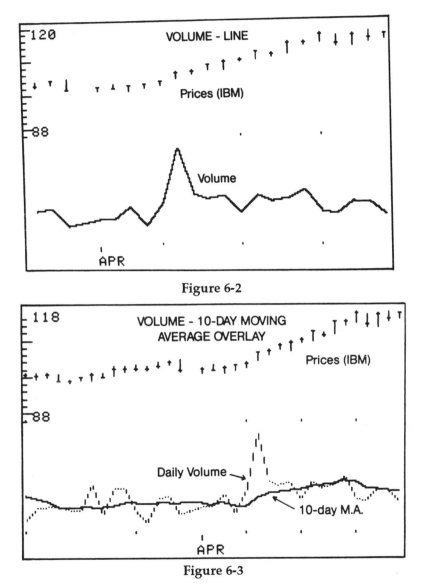

Figure 6-2

Figure 6-3

In sum, an understanding of volume patterns adds a third dimension to our analysis. Now we're ready to begin to apply these concepts to key patterns which appear on our charts.

# REVERSAL PATTERNS

In Chapter 5, we noted that one way to tell if a trend has changed is to watch for a breaking of the trendline; and in Chapter 6 we saw how volume patterns may or may not confirm this change. Further investigation would show us that when a price trend is in the process of reversal—either from up to down or from down to up—a *characteristic pattern* takes shape on the chart and becomes recognizable as a "reversal formation."

**THE HEAD AND SHOULDERS TOP** formation is one of the most common and also one of the most reliable of all the major reversal patterns.

It consists of a left shoulder, a head and a right shoulder.

*The left shoulder* is formed usually at the end of an extensive advance during which volume is quite heavy. At the end of the left shoulder, there is usually a small dip or recession which typically occurs on low volume.

*The head* then forms with heavy volume on the upside and with lesser volume accompanying the subsequent reaction. At this point, in order to conform to proper form, prices must come down some-

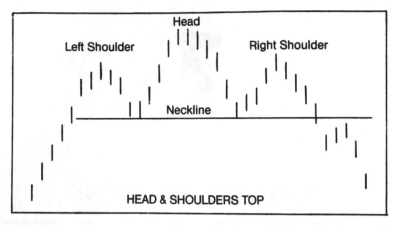

Figure 7-1

where *near* the low of the left shoulder—somewhat lower perhaps or somewhat higher but, in any case, below the top of the left shoulder.

*The right shoulder* is then formed by a rally on usually less volume than any previous rallies in this formation.

*A neckline* can now be drawn across the bottoms of the left shoulder, the head and right shoulder. A breaking of this neckline on a decline from the right shoulder is the final confirmation and completes the Head and Shoulders Top formation. This is, therefore, your signal to sell short.

A word of caution. Very often, after moving lower, prices will pull back to the neckline before continuing their descent. You may wait for this pullback to sell or use it as a point to add to your original short positions.

Most Head and Shoulders are not perfectly symmetrical. One shoulder may appear to droop. Also, the time involved in the development of each shoulder may vary, causing the structure to lose symmetry. The neckline, rather than being horizontal, may be sloping up or down. The only qualification on an up-sloping neckline is that the lowest point on the right shoulder must be appreciably lower than that of the top of the left shoulder.

A Head and Shoulders formation can also be extremely useful in estimating the probable extent of the move once the neckline has been penetrated.

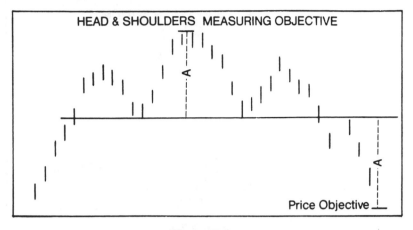

**Figure 7-2**

Here's what you do: Referring to Figure 7-2, measure the distance vertically from the top of the head to the neckline. Then measure the same distance down from the point where prices penetrated the neckline (following the completion of the right shoulder). This gives you the minimum objective of how far prices should decline following the successful completion of the Head and Shoulders Top. To double check your estimate, one guideline to look at is the extent of the previous rise. If the up move preceding the Head and Shoulders Top has been small, the ensuing down move may be small as well. Thus, the extent of the previous advance should be at least as large as the objective you have estimated from the formation.

**THE HEAD AND SHOULDERS BOTTOM** formation is simply the inverse of a Head and Shoulders Top, and often indicates a trend reversal from down to up. The typical Head and Shoulders Bottom formation is illustrated in Figure 7-3.

The volume pattern is somewhat different in a Head and Shoulders Bottom and should be watched carefully. Volume should pick up as prices rally from the bottom of the head and then increase even more dramatically on the rally from the right shoulder. If the breaking of the neckline is done on low volume we must be suspect of this formation. The breakout could be false, only to be followed by a retest of the lows. A high volume breakout, on the other hand, would

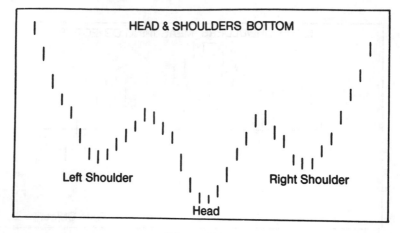

Figure 7-3

give us good reason to believe the Head and Shoulders Bottom formation is genuine.

The only other noticeable difference in the Head and Shoulders Bottom formation is that it may sometimes appear flatter than the Head and Shoulders Top. Often the turns are more rounded. Otherwise, all the rules and measuring objectives can be applied equally well.

**DOUBLE TOP FORMATIONS** appear as an "M" on a chart as in Figure 7-4. They are very "popular." But watch out! Many analysts often mislabel and misinterpret Double Top and Bottom formations. In any uptrend, after a reaction, each new wave up will appear to be "making" a Double Top (see Figure 7-5).

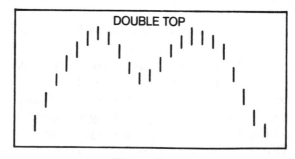

Figure 7-4

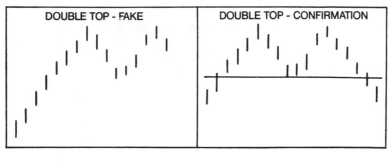

**Figure 7-5**                    **Figure 7-6**

But in truth, at this point there is *absolutely no evidence pointing to a Double Top*. Nine times out of ten, the trend will remain in force and prices will simply go on to make new highs. So don't be fooled. You have no confirmation whatsoever of a Double Top until the valley has been broken as in Figure 7-6.

Volume, again, can offer a clue in the formation of this pattern. If the volume on the rise of the second peak is less than on the first peak, you have an initial indication that prices may fail to go above the previous high, turn around and go on to confirm the Double Top. High volume accompanying the second rise would minimize that possibility.

Another factor to use in determining the validity of a Double Top formation is the time element. If two tops appear at the same level but quite close together in time, the chances are good that they are merely part of a consolidation area. If, on the other hand, the peaks are separated by a deep and long reaction, this is more likely a true Double Top:

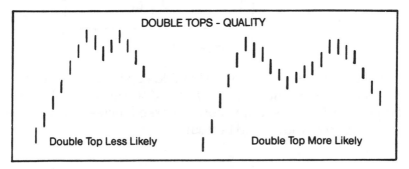

**Figure 7-7**

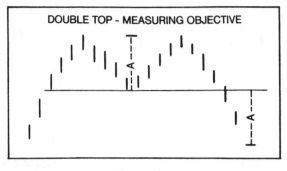

**Figure 7-8**

As with the Head and Shoulders formation, a pullback to the valley area is very possible. If you wish to measure the objective from the breakout point, you can simply take the distance from peak to valley and subtract from the valley to the "M" as in Figure 7-8.

**DOUBLE BOTTOMS** are the inverse of Double Tops and appear on the charts as a W formation:

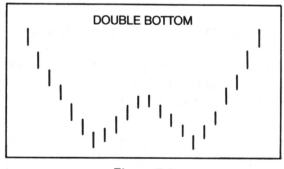

**Figure 7-9**

All of the rules associated with Double Top formations also apply to Double Bottoms. The volume patterns, of course, are different. A valid Double Bottom should show a marked increase in volume on the rally up from the second bottom.

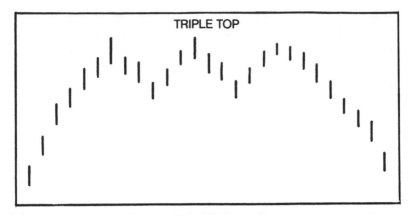

**Figure 7-10**

**TRIPLE TOPS** are more rare than Double Tops. They appear on a chart similar to the pattern shown in Figure 7-10.

Volume is usually less on the second advance, and still less on the third. The highs need not be spaced as far apart as those which constitute a Double Top, and they need not be equally spaced. Also, the intervening valleys need not bottom out at exactly the same level; either the first or the second may be deeper. But the triple top is not confirmed until prices have broken through both valleys.

There are several different trading strategies that can be employed to take advantage of the Triple Top formation. After a Double Top has been confirmed, if prices are rallying again but on light volume, it is a good place to sell short with a stop (exit point) above the highest peak of the Double Top (Figure 7-11)

Another good place to sell would be after a Triple Top has formed and a fourth lower top is being formed.

If, however, prices continue to rally up to the level of the three previous peaks, they usually go higher; and if prices descend to the same level a fourth time, they usually go lower. It is very rare to see four tops or bottoms at equal levels.

**TRIPLE BOTTOMS** are simply Triple Tops turned upside down and all the rules can be applied in reverse. (Figure 7-12).

The accompanying volume pattern, however, is different. The

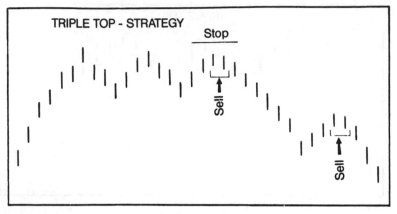

**Figure 7-11**

third low should be on light volume and the ensuing rally from that bottom should show a considerable pickup in activity.

**ROUNDING TOPS AND BOTTOMS**. Because Rounding Tops are so rare, we will limit our discussion to Rounding Bottoms, commonly referred to as "Saucer Bottoms."

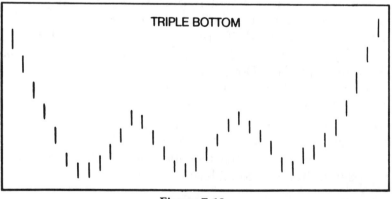

**Figure 7-12**

The chart pattern in Figure 7-13 shows a gradual change in the trend direction, produced by a step-by-step shift in the balance of power between buying and selling. As we begin a Rounded Bottom,

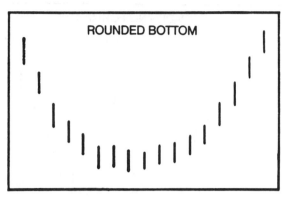

**Figure 7-13**

we will notice volume decreasing as selling pressure eases. The trend then becomes neutral with very little trading activity occurring. As prices start up, volume increases as well. Finally, price and volume continue to accelerate, with prices often literally blasting out of this pattern.

**BROADENING FORMATIONS**, such as the one illustrated in Figure 7-14 usually have bearish implications. They appear much more frequently at tops than at bottoms and, for that reason, we will limit our discussion to Broadening Tops. The theory is that *five minor reversals are followed by a substantial decline*. In the classic pattern, reversals #3 and #5 occur at successively higher points than reversal #1; and reversal #4 occurs at a lower point than reversal #2. This same characteristic pattern was evident on many individual stocks in the third quarter of 1929, preceding the great crash.

The Broadening Top formation usually suggests a market that is lacking support from the "smart money" and is out of control. Quite often, well-informed selling is completed during the early stages of the formation; and in the later stages, the participation is from the less-informed, more excitable public. Volume is often very irregular and offers no clue as to the direction of the subsequent breakout. The price swings themselves are very unpredictable so that it is difficult to tell where each swing will end.

Broadening Tops are a difficult formation to trade. However, you

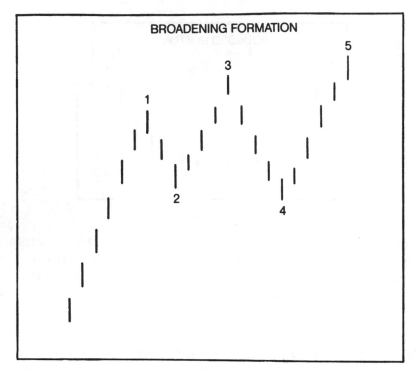

**Figure 7-14**

can usually be quite sure the trend has turned down after a break of the lower of the two valleys.

**WEDGE FORMATIONS.** Up until now, the reversal formations we have discussed have all been powerful enough to reverse an intermediate or major trend. The Wedges, on the other hand, usually only reverse a *minor* trend and, as a general rule of thumb, should typically take three weeks or so to complete. It is a chart formation in which price fluctuations are confined within converging straight lines. These form a pattern which itself may have a rising or falling slant.

In a **RISING WEDGE**, both boundary lines slant up from left to right but the lower line rises at a steeper angle than the upper line. After breaking the lower line boundary, prices usually decline in earnest (Figure 7-15).

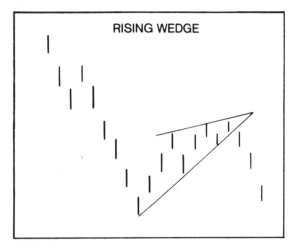

**Figure 7-15**

Generally, each new price advance, or wave up, is feebler than the last, indicating that investment demand is weakening at the higher price levels. Rising Wedges are usually more reliable when found in a Bear Market. In a Bull Market, what appears to be a Rising Wedge may actually be a continuation pattern known as a "Flag" or "Pennant" (discussed in the next chapter). This is more likely to be true if the Wedge is less than three weeks in length.

In a **FALLING WEDGE,** both boundary lines slant down from right to left but the upper line descends at a steeper angle than the lower line. Differing from the Rising Wedge, once prices move out of a Falling Wedge, they are more apt to drift sidewise and "saucer-out" before beginning to rise. (Figure 7-16).

## Minor Reversal Patterns

**A REVERSAL DAY TOP** occurs when prices move higher but then close near the lows of the day, usually below their opening and below the mid-point of the day's range. An even stronger reversal is indicated if the close is below the previous day's close. (Figure 7-17).

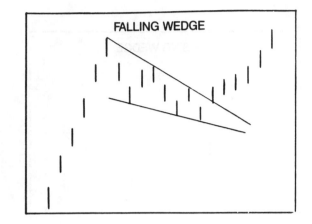

Figure 7-16

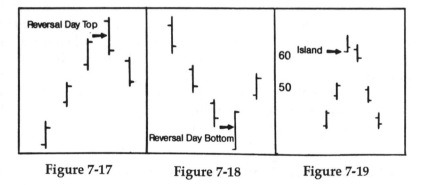

Figure 7-17          Figure 7-18          Figure 7-19

**A REVERSAL DAY BOTTOM** occurs when prices move lower but then close near the highs of the day, usually above the opening and above the mid-point of the day's range. An even stronger reversal is indicated if the close is above the previous day's close. (Figure 7-18).

**THE ISLAND REVERSAL.** Suppose the price of a stock in a rising market closes at its high of 50 and then on the following day, opens at its low of 60, leaving a "gap" of 10 points (see Chapter 9). A few days later, the market moves back down and forms another gap in approximately the same 50-60 area. Thus, all the trading above 60 will appear on the chart to be *isolated*, like an island, from all previous and subsequent fluctuations. This is called an "island reversal."

Island Reversals are quite rare, but are an extremely good indicator of a reversal in the trend. Their appearance indicates that an extreme change in sentiment has occurred.

Thus, we have seen various patterns which can often signal a critical change in market direction. In the chapter to follow, you will see various formations which give you precisely the opposite indication. We recommend you compare these chapters carefully and bear in mind the key differences between these formations whenever making a trading decision.

# CONSOLIDATION PATTERNS

We have seen how trends are reversed. But at other times, a trend may be interrupted, resulting in sideways movement for a time, before continuing on in its previous direction. Such sideways movements may even result in a break of the trendline. These formations are known as "consolidation" or "continuation patterns." The ability to differentiate between reversal patterns and continuation patterns is vital.

**TRIANGLES** have occasionally been known to reverse a trend. But usually they act as a period of consolidation from which prices continue on in the same direction. Triangles form as a result of indecision on the part of both buyers and sellers. During this time, market participants tend to withdraw to the sidelines, resulting in narrower market fluctuations and diminishing volume. A breakout of the triangle usually occurs as the result of some news affecting the market. And this breakout, if legitimate, is accompanied by a sharp increase in volume.

**THE SYMMETRICAL TRIANGLE,** sometimes known as a "coil," is the most common type. It is formed by a succession of price

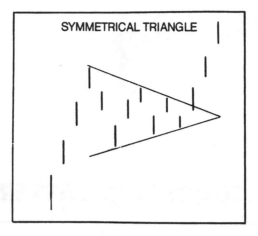

Figure 8-1

fluctuations, each of which is smaller than its predecessor, resulting in a pattern bounded by a downslanting line and an upslanting line. (Figure 8-1).

A Symmetrical Triangle, by definition, must have at least four reversal points. From that point onward, the breakout may occur at any time in the triangle, even before reaching its apex. More powerful moves are found when prices break out decisively at a point somewhere between half and three-quarters of the distance between the left side of the triangle and the apex.

Symmetrical Triangles are not as reliable as the Head and Shoulders formations, and really work out only about two-thirds of the

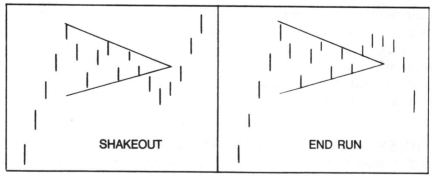

Figure 8-2                              Figure 8-3

time because they are subject to false breakouts called "End Runs" or "Shakeouts" (Figure 8-2 and Figure 8-3).

There is no way to avoid getting caught in such false moves—unless you recognize their characteristic volume patterns. A breakout to the upside should be on high volume. If volume is light, be suspect of a possible false move and "End Run."

Downside breakouts are a different matter. Prices often break out on low volume with a pickup in volume not occurring for a few days. Oddly enough, a high-volume breakout on the downside is often the signal of a "Shakeout."

**RIGHT-ANGLE TRIANGLES,** both Ascending and Descending, are better predictors of the future directions of prices than Symmetrical Triangles. In theory, prices will break toward the flat side—upward in an Ascending Triangle and downward in a Descending Triangle.

**THE ASCENDING RIGHT-ANGLE TRIANGLE** is characterized by a top-line boundary that is horizontal and a bottom-line that is sloping upward (Figure 8-4).

This formation occurs when demand is growing yet continues to meet supply at a fixed price. If demand continues, the supply being distributed at that price will eventually be entirely absorbed by new buyers, and prices will then advance rapidly.

**THE DESCENDING RIGHT-ANGLE TRIANGLE** will exhibit a horizontal lower boundary and a down-sloping upper boundary (Figure 8-4 and Figure 8-5).

This formation occurs when there is a certain amount of demand at a fixed price yet supply continues to come into the market. Eventually, the demand is exhausted and prices break out of a triangle on the downside.

Triangles, both Symmetrical and Right-Angle, can be used for some measuring though they are not as reliable as the Head-and-Shoulders measuring formula. Assuming, for example, a breakout

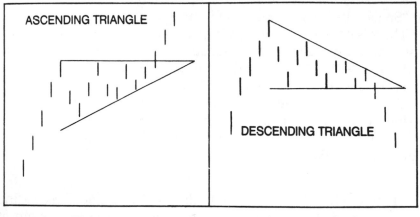

Figure 8-4                    Figure 8-5

on the upside, you simply draw a line parallel to the lower side of the triangle and expect prices to rally up to that line (Figure 8-6).

Also, prices should resume their uptrend at the same approximate angle as the uptrend which preceded the triangle's formation.

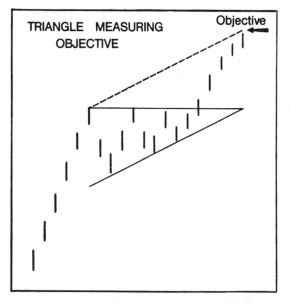

Figure 8-6

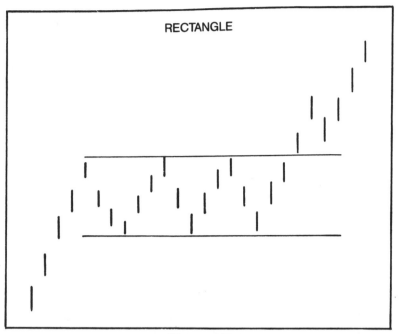

**Figure 8-7**

**THE RECTANGLE** formation, sometimes known as a "line," forms as a result of a battle between two groups of approximately equal strength. Although offering little forecasting ability as to which direction the breakout should occur, once prices begin to move out of the formation, it can be very useful in setting objectives (Figure 8-7).

Volume characteristics are similar to triangles in that volume tends to diminish as the Rectangle lengthens. Breakouts have less tendency to be false than with the Symmetrical Triangles. However, breakouts are more likely to be followed by a pullback.

All in all, there is a somewhat greater tendency for Rectangles to be consolidation rather than reversal patterns. When a Rectangle is a reversal pattern, it is much more likely to occur at a major or intermediate bottom rather than at a top.

A minimum measuring objective can be derived from adding the width of the Rectangle to the point of breakout. Normally, wide-swinging Rectangles will offer more dynamic moves than the nar-

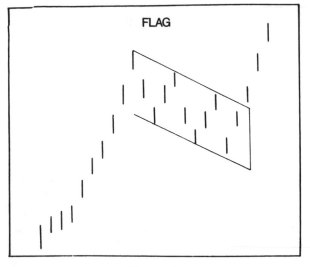

**Figure 8-8**

rower ones. A move out of a narrow Rectangle will often hesitate at its minimum objective before moving on.

**FLAGS AND PENNANTS** are true consolidation patterns and are very reliable indicators both in terms of direction and measuring. In an up market, flags usually form after a dynamic, nearly straight move up on heavy volume. Prices react on lower volume and a series of minor fluctuations eventually form a downward-sloping, compact parallelogram (Figure 8-8).

The pennant is very similar to the flag except that it is bounded by converging rather than parallel lines (Figure 8-9).

Flags and pennants, in order to be considered valid should conform to three rules—(1) they should occur after a very sharp up or down move; (2) volume should decline throughout the duration of the pattern; and (3) prices should break out of the pattern within a matter of a few weeks.

The measuring formula for flags and pennants is identical. You simply add the height of the "pole," formed in the move preceding the formation, to the breakout point of the flag (Figure 8-10).

In practice, price may tend to overshoot this objective somewhat

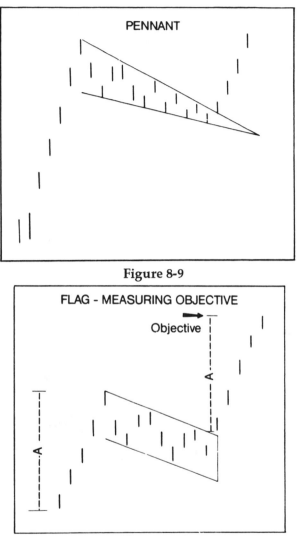

**Figure 8-9**

**Figure 8-10**

in an advancing market, while falling short of the objective in a declining market.

All of these patterns help confirm a trend. But looking more closely at market fluctuations, we notice another phenomenon which can also give us additional clues—gaps. This is the subject of our next chapter.

# 9

## GAPS

---

Gaps represent an area on the chart where no trading takes place. For example, if a stock reaches a high of, say, 50 on Monday, but then opens at 60 on Tuesday, moving straight up from the opening, no trading occurs in the 50-60 area. This no-trading zone appears on the chart as a hole or a "gap." Thus, in an uptrending market, a gap is produced when the highest price of any one day is lower than the lowest price of the following day, or the reverse in a downtrending market.

Gaps can be valuable in spotting the beginning of a move, measuring the extent of a move or confirming the end of a move. There are four different types of gaps: "Common gaps," "breakaway gaps," "measuring gaps," and "exhaustion gaps." Since each has its own distinctive implications, it is important to be able to distinguish between them.

COMMON GAPS—also known as "temporary gaps," "pattern gaps" or "area gaps"—tend to occur in a sideways trading range or price congestion area. Usually, the price moves back up or down subsequently as the market returns to the gap area in order to "fill the gap." If this does occur, the gap offers little in the way of forecasting significance.

It may be noted, however, that common gaps are more apt to develop in consolidation rather than in reversal formations. In other words, the appearance of many gaps within consolidation patterns (such as a Rectangle or Symmetrical Triangle) is a signal that the breakout should be in the same direction as that of the preceding trend (Figure 9-1).

**THE BREAKAWAY GAP** occurs as prices break away from an area of congestion. Typically, prices will break away from an Ascending or Descending Triangle with a gap.

This gap implies that the change in sentiment has been strong and that the ensuing move will be powerful. Often the market does not return to "fill the gap," particularly if volume is heavy after the gap has formed. If volume is not heavy, there is a reasonable chance the gap will be filled before prices resume their trend (Figure 9-2).

**THE MEASURING GAP** typically occurs in the middle of a price move and can be used to measure how much farther a move will go. Rather than being associated with a congestion area, it is more likely to occur in the course of a rapid, straight-line advance or decline, usually at approximately the halfway point (Figure 9-3).

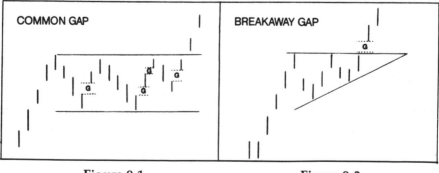

Figure 9-1     Figure 9-2

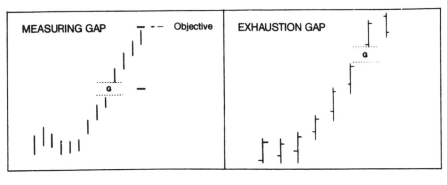

Figure 9-3                         Figure 9-4

**THE EXHAUSTION GAP** signals the end of a move. Like Measuring Gaps, Exhaustion Gaps are associated with rapid, extensive advances or declines. The problem, of course, is: how do you know whether it's a Measuring Gap or an Exhaustion Gap? One clue may be found in the volume. An Exhaustion gap is often accompanied by particularly high volume. Another method for detecting an Exhaustion Gap is with a Reversal Day (Figure 9-4).

Now, combining the concepts of the past several chapters, we have numerous tools for deciding when a market could be turning. The next question which arises is: How far will it go? Chapter 10 begins to provide some answers.

# 10

# RETRACEMENT THEORY

No market moves steadily down or steadily up. Instead, each movement in the primary direction is followed by a reaction, which can,
in turn, be followed by another thrust.

Each thrust, measured from bottom to top or top to bottom, is
known as the "swing" or "move." Each reaction or rally retraces part
of the move and, therefore, is known as a "retracement." When the
reaction is greater than the move, we must consider that the trend
has changed, at least, for the near term. Retracement theory sets
predetermined target levels for these moves and lends itself readily
to computer applications.

Of course, our first problem is to determine the primary trend.
But once we are reasonably assured that the market is in a downtrend
or an uptrend, the key is to know how far a move is likely to be
retraced before the market resumes that trend. Knowing that, we
could better judge an appropriate point to enter the market on a
reaction. Aside from correctly judging the primary trend, correctly
timing entries on reactions is probably the most important aspect of
trading.

What is a "normal" retracement? This question has been debated
for years. The general consensus is that a normal retracement recap-

tures between one-third and two-thirds of the previous move. Another school of thought says 40-60 percent. Most agree that the 50 percent retracement is the most likely.

W.D. Gann went as far as to divide each move into eighths and thirds, giving us 1/8, 1/4, 3/8, 1/3, 1/2, 5/8, 2/3, 3/4, and 7/8 as all possible retracement levels. Of these, the most important to him were the 1/2, 5/8, 3/4 and 7/8 levels. Meanwhile, students of Elliott Wave Theory consider the Fibonacci retracement levels of .382 and .618 to be the most critical. My own work shows special significance attached to these numbers, especially the .618; and often I've seen markets react exactly to this level before moving on.

Therefore, on your charts, it would be a good idea to keep track of some of the significant retracement levels such as in Figure 10-1.

Keep in mind that each "move" is part of a larger move that has its own individual probable retracement levels. Consequently, you may want to go back and look at the current entire pattern in an even broader, longer-term perspective, viewing it as merely a retracement within the context of an even larger move.

Often, you will find key retracement levels of different moves coinciding with one another, lending more credibility to your forecast that the market will indeed find support at that level.

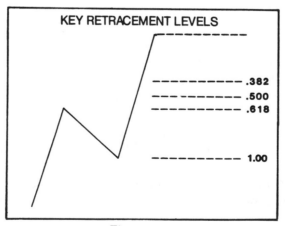

**Figure 10-1**

# 11

# SUPPORT AND RESISTANCE

In addition to any retracement theory, what are some other ways of judging when a reaction or rally is coming to an end and when the primary trend should resume? Support and resistance will give you some clues.

**A SUPPORT LEVEL** is a price level at which sufficient demand exists to at least temporarily halt a downward movement in prices.

**A RESISTANCE LEVEL** is a price at which sufficient supply exists to at least temporarily halt an upward movement.

In an uptrend, each former top—once surpassed—becomes a support level. In a downtrend, each former bottom—once penetrated—becomes a resistance level (Figure 11-1 and Figure 11-2).

A congestion pattern forms an even more formidable support of resistance barrier since more actual trading took place at that price level (Figure 11-3 and Figure 11-4).

One more rule to remember: When a support level is broken, it becomes resistance, and when a resistance level is broken, it becomes support. How does this happen?

Let's take the hypothetical situation illustrated in Figure 11-5. A

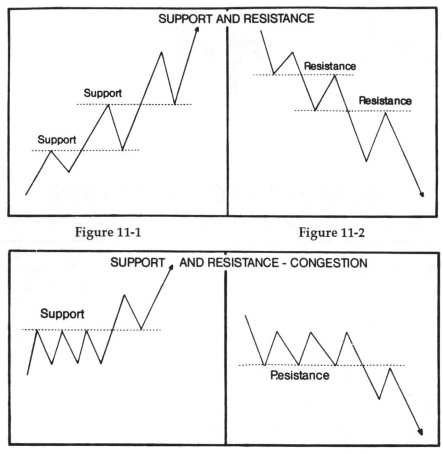

Figure 11-1                    Figure 11-2

Figure 11-3                    Figure 11-4

group of buyers has been waiting on the sidelines and watching a stock decline from 80 to 60. At this price, they believe the stock is cheap so they buy. The stock begins to rise and eventually reaches 70. But they are confident the stock will go much higher. Unfortunately, the stock begins to decline and eventually falls to 50. At this point, the investors begin to feel they have made a mistake and vow to dump the stock if they can at least get their money back. Luckily, the stock begins to rally and as it reaches 60, these investors sell their shares, turning the stock price down once again.

Months pass. Our same group of investors find a hot new stock— ABC Company (refer to Figure 11-6). They buy it at 10 and, after a

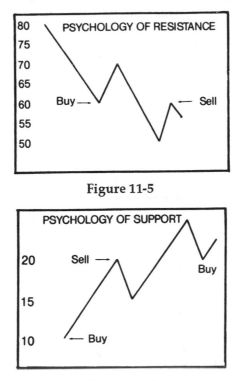

**Figure 11-5**

**Figure 11-6**

few months, the stock has risen to 20. This time they don't repeat the same mistake they made earlier. Instead, they sell the stock and pocket a huge profit. Two weeks later, the stock has dropped to 15 and they congratulate themselves for having taken their profits at 20. But a month later, the price of ABC has risen to 25. Now they don't feel so smart. "Maybe we should have held on longer for even more profit," is their refrain. They decide that if they get another chance to buy the stock again at 20, they will. This is one example of how previous tops can act as support.

In Figure 11-1, we showed a typical zigzag type of market, i.e., where each reaction found support at the previous top. Referring to Figures 11-7 and 11-8, there are two other possibilities that can come up. A market may surge wildly, in which case we would not expect a reaction to take prices back to the previous top. Instead, on reaction,

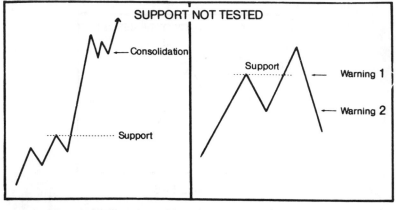

Figure 11-7                         Figure 11-8

prices are likely to form a consolidation or reversal pattern some-what above the price level of the previous top.

Another possibility is that prices break below their previous top, giving you your first warning signal of a change in direction, with a stronger warning occurring if prices break below their previous bottom.

Before leaving the subject of support and resistance, we should state one final rule: Once a support or resistance level has been attacked, it is weakened. It may resist a second attack, but the third attack will usually break through.

# 12

## MOMENTUM

Momentum is simply the rate of change—the *speed* or *slope* at which a stock or commodity ascends or declines. It is calculated by taking the difference between prices separated by a fixed interval of time. For example, today's five-day momentum value would be today's price minus the price recorded five days ago; yesterday's would be yesterday's price minus that of five days before yesterday and so on. Expressed mathematically:

$$M(5)_T = \text{Price of today} - \text{price of 5 days ago}$$
$$\text{or } M(5)_T = P_T - P_{T-5}$$

Let's take a hypothetical example:

| DAY | PRICE | 5-DAY MOMENTUM |
|-----|-------|----------------|
| 1 | 500 | — |
| 2 | 508 | — |
| 3 | 510 | — |
| 4 | 515 | — |
| 5 | 510 | — |
| 6 | 495 | –5 |
| 7 | 508 | 0 |
| 8 | 526 | 16 |
| 9 | 528 | 13 |
| 10 | 540 | 30 |

One basic way to use a momentum indicator is to buy when it becomes positive and sell when it turns negative. Logically, you are buying when the market is picking up momentum and selling when that momentum is lost. The problem is that, by definition, you're entering the market *after* it has made its turn. But even if you miss the beginning of the move, you should catch most of it, if indeed the market is turning. Later, this should also allow you to exit the market with a profit before prices actually start moving against you in earnest:

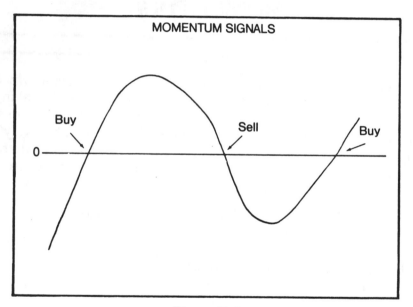

**Figure 12-1**

**CYCLES AND MOMENTUM.** One school of thought contends that in order for a momentum indicator to be valid, it must be based on *cycle length*. If it is, it will measure the rate of change of prices within a cycle.

Cycles are found by measuring from one bottom to the next. Cycles are sometimes consistent and easy to spot while at other times they are very difficult to find. Let us assume we have checked on the recent history of a market and have found that it consistently makes a bottom every 20 days or so. The rule states that our calculation of momentum should be set at one-half the days in the cycle, or in this case, 10 days.

This concept can be taken even further by following *three* momentum indicators at the same time—the 10-day momentum *plus* one at 1/4 of the cycle (5 days) and one at the full cycle (20 days). Thus, you will be plotting a 5-day, 10-day and 20-day momentum simultaneously on the same graph. (For more on cycles, see Chapters 23, 24 and 25.)

Up to this point, we can summarize the theory of momentum indicators as follows:

### Rising Prices:

1.  When the momentum indicator is above zero and moving up, *upward momentum is increasing.*

2.  When the momentum indicator is above zero and moving down, *upward momentum is decreasing.*

### Declining Prices:

3.  When the momentum indicator is below zero and moving down, *downward momentum is increasing.*

4.  When the momentum indicator is below zero and moving up, *downward momentum is decreasing.*

**OSCILLATORS.** A completely different approach to the use of momentum indicators attempts to anticipate the end of a move when momentum is either "too high" or "too low." These conditions, respectively, are known as "overbought" and "oversold." The idea is that, in an overbought condition, nearly all investors who have had any intention of buying this particular stock or commodity have probably *already* committed all or most of the money they intend to commit for the time being; while in an oversold condition, they have *already* done most of their selling. The general rule is to sell when the momentum indicator shows an overbought reading and buy when an oversold condition is indicated (Figure 12-2).

Momentum may be zero, positive or negative. If a market is at the same price after five days, the five-day momentum will be zero. If it is higher, the momentum is positive; and if lower, negative. The key question is this: *Is there a maximum positive or negative value for momentum?* In commodity markets the answer is *yes.* There is usually a specified, mandatory limit as to how much a price is allowed to move each day. So, in this case, the maximum five-day momentum would generally be that daily limit multiplied by five.

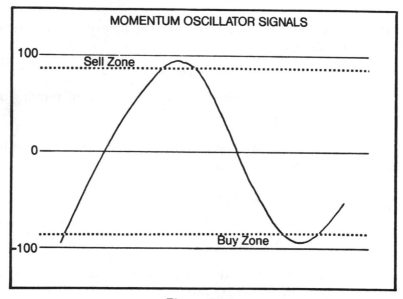

**Figure 12-2**

A momentum indicator used in this way is referred to as an "oscillator." The momentum indicator we have been discussing, however, is not an oscillator in its present form. It must first be "normalized," which means that all values must be converted to a range between +1 and -1, or +100 percent and -100 percent. To accomplish this, we divided the momentum value by the maximum obtainable momentum value. For example, in the T-bill market, the limit for one day is 60 points. Using a five-day momentum would give us a maximum obtainable momentum of 300. Thus, a momentum value of 150 would translate into an oscillator value of +0.5 or +50 percent.

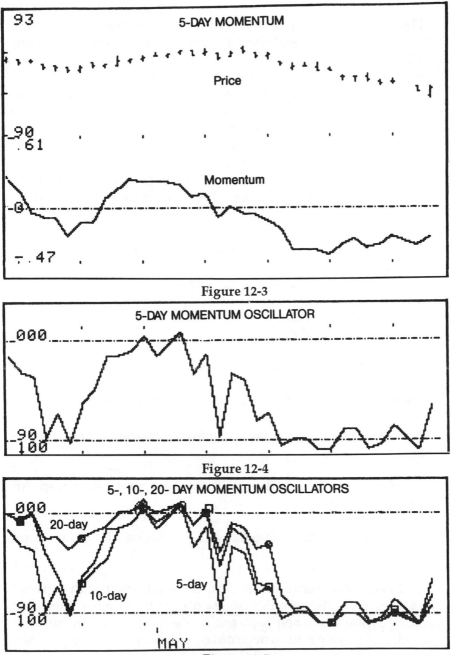

Figure 12-3

Figure 12-4

Figure 12-5

Figures 12-3, 12-4 and 12-5 show a 5-day momentum, a 5-day momentum oscillator, and combined 5-, 10- and 20-day momentum oscillators.

Bear in mind that any limit we set—whether based upon actual market limits or not—is an arbitrary guideline to give you a general idea of the overbought or oversold condition. A more valid way to set limits is to run the momentum indicator for approximately one year of history and use the indicator's highs and lows of that period as your maximum and minimum.

It is very easy, with a computer to develop a trading system using overbought/oversold oscillators. These would be the logical steps to follow:

1.   Select how many days to use for momentum.

2.   Decide on one or more oscillators.

3.   Define the maximum ranges—what will constitute an overbought or oversold condition.

4.   Construct trading rules.

Some examples of different trading rules might be:

1.   Sell when the five-day oscillator goes above 0.9 or 90 percent.

2.   Sell when the five-day oscillator stays above 90 percent for two days.

3.   Sell when both the five-day and ten-day oscillators are above 90 percent.

In short, momentum indicators can be used to trade with the trend when they cross the zero line or against the trend when they hit a peak. Be aware that when you are either selling into an overbought condition or buying into an oversold condition, you are categorically bucking the short-term trend. You are betting on what your oscillators claim is a high probability of a technical reaction occurring. Accordingly, this type of method is best suited to very short-term trading. In developing a trading system based on momentum, I would prefer to trade *with* the trend. Overbought/oversold oscillators do, however, provide indispensable technical information to the analyst—I wouldn't be without them.

# 13

# MOVING AVERAGES

Moving averages are used to determine when a trend has changed direction and are the basis of many trend-following systems. In a simple three-day moving average, for example, we add the three most recent days and divided by three. Thus, if today is Wednesday, the moving average for today would be the average price of Monday, Tuesday and Wednesday. Then, on Thursday, we would drop off Monday's price and take the average of Tuesday, Wednesday and Thursday; and so on. The formula for a simple three-day moving average (M3) would be:

$$M3 = \frac{P_T + P_{T-1} + P_{T-2}}{3}$$

When $P_T$ equals today's close; $P_{T-1}$ equals yesterday's close; and $P_{T-2}$ equals the close of the day before yesterday. Table 13-1 shows a hypothetical example:

### TABLE 13-1. BUILDING A 3-DAY MOVING AVERAGE

| Day | Price | 3-Day Moving Average |
|:---:|:---:|:---:|
| 1 | 5 | — |
| 2 | 6 | — |
| 3 | 7 | 6 |
| 4 | 9 | 7.33 |
| 5 | 11 | 9 |

The simple moving average gives equal weight to each price in the sample.

**A WEIGHTED MOVING AVERAGE** on the other hand, can be used to give more significance to the most recent price, the earliest price or the middle price in the group. Another popular type of weighting factor is known as *exponential smoothing* which can be calculated for you automatically with a computer.

Prepackaged software is readily available to compute both simple and exponentially-smoothed moving averages. In addition, such software usually lets you set the number of days (or weeks or months as the case may be) in the moving average. As the number of days in the moving average increases, the moving average becomes smoother, less responsive to short-term fluctuations and, thus, slower to respond to changes in trend. The advantage is that you will experience fewer false starts; and the primary disadvantage is that much of the price move will have already taken place by the time the slow moving average has signaled a change. Your diligent research in this area will tell you which moving average shows optimum results for each stock or commodity you wish to trade. This is the first step toward developing a moving average system.

### Moving Average Systems

A moving average is a set of trading rules that are applied to moving averages. On the same chart you may be interested in:

(a)    the relationship between price and moving average, or

(b)    the relationship between two or more moving averages themselves.

The most basic way to use a moving average is to simply interpret a change of direction in a single moving average as a signal to buy or sell (Figure 13-1).

However, this is perhaps *too* simple. A more common approach would be to study the relationship between actual price and a single moving average. In the stock market, when a stock price is above its 200-day moving average, it is considered a bullish sign. (Shorter-term signals would be generated using a 10- or 20-day moving average.) The basic strategy would be as follows: Buy when prices cross *above* the moving average. Sell when prices cross *below* the moving average. Typically, you may wish to use closing prices only (Figure 13-2).

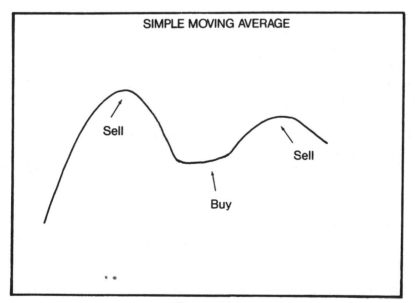

**Figure 13-1**

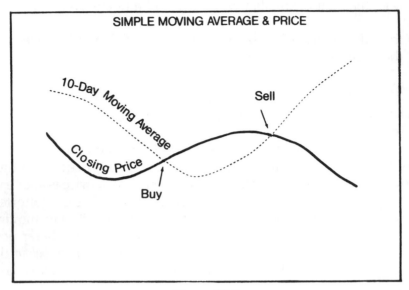

**Figure 13-2**

**THE TWO CROSSOVER MODEL** is the next step up in level of complexity, making use of two simple moving averages. A typical example would be a 14-day moving average combined with a 50-day moving average. (This particular combination was found to be very effective in the gold market in a study done by Merrill Lynch.) The rule would be: Buy when the 14-day moving average crosses above the 50-day moving average; sell when it crosses below the 50-day moving average.

A modified version of this system would take into account the actual prices as well. The rules might then be:

(1)   Buy when the actual price crosses above *both* moving averages and exit the market when the price crosses below   *either* moving average.

(2)   Sell short when the actual price crosses below *both* moving averages and exit the market when the price crosses *above either moving average.*

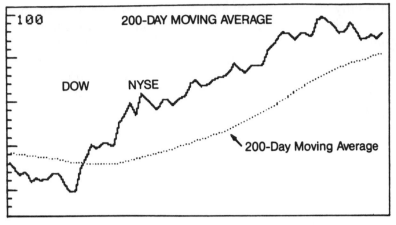

**Figure 13-3**

Finally, three or more moving averages may be combined to make a system. Such qualifications usually result in fewer trades and trades of a shorter duration. Moreover, it is probably too complex. Remember, making a system more complex does not necessarily make it a better one.

**THE 200-DAY MOVING AVERAGE OF THE DOW** illustrated in Figure 13-3, is an excellent long-term indicator, and as such may be better utilized by the investor rather than the trader. Its signals, once generated, are seldom wrong over the longer term. If, after both the Dow and the 200-Day Moving Average have been declining for some time, the Dow should move up and cross the Moving Average, it indicates that a new bull market has begun. Later, confirmation of this initial signal occurs when the 200-Day Moving Average itself turns up.

During the first stage of the bull market, both the Dow and the Moving Average move up in concert. Eventually, the Dow suffers its first serious setback which may or may not send prices below the Moving Average. But this does not necessarily signal an end to the bull market. If the market correction is severe, the Moving Average may turn down as well. Again, this does not necessarily mean the bull market has ended. Instead, the Moving Average will usually turn back and go on to new highs.

It is only *after* this *second* leg up in the 200-Day Moving Average that you should begin to look for market deterioration and sell signals—an initial crossing *below* the Moving Average by the Dow and then, a decline in the Moving Average itself.

All these moving averages ignore volume. Attempts to evaluate both *price* and volume simultaneously are discussed in the next chapter.

# 14

# ON-BALANCE VOLUME

Earlier, just as studying volume on a day-to-day basis helped us to determine the power of a particular price move, so does On-Balance Volume (OBV) help us to detect patterns of accumulation and distribution.

**JOSEPH GRANVILLE** calculates it this way: If today's closing price is higher than yesterday's, we add today's volume to a cumulative total. If the closing price is lower, today's volume is subtracted from the total. On days when prices remain unchanged, the cumulative volume also remains unchanged. Here is an example to illustrate the technique:

TABLE 14-1. CALCULATING ON-BALANCE VOLUME

| Day | Price | Volume | On-Balance Volume |
|-----|-------|--------|-------------------|
| 1 | 10 | 7,000 | 7,000 |
| 2 | 12 | 5,000 | 12,000 |
| 3 | 15 | 8,000 | 20,000 |
| 4 | 15 | 4,000 | 20,000 |
| 5 | 14 | 5,000 | 15,000 |
| 6 | 12 | 3,000 | 12,000 |

On-Balance Volume can be equally effective with individual stocks, the stock averages, or individual commodities. Accumulation is indicated by rising OBV; distribution by falling OBV. Since the starting point is arbitrary, the absolute level of the on-balance volume is of no significance. We are only interested in the contour of its curve when it is compared with the contour of the price curve—either graphically or in tabulated form.

For example, let's say prices are moving sideways. Is this an accumulation which will lead to a continuation of the trend? Or is it a distribution which implies that prices will turn around and move in the opposite direction? The OBV can often tell us the true state of affairs. As a rule, the OBV parallels the price. It is only when there is a *divergence* between the OBV and the price that we can tell if accumulation or distribution is occurring. For example, if prices have been moving sideways in a trading range while OBV has been increasing, we would conclude that accumulation was occurring. The rising OBV resulted from more stock being purchased on up days than was sold on down days:

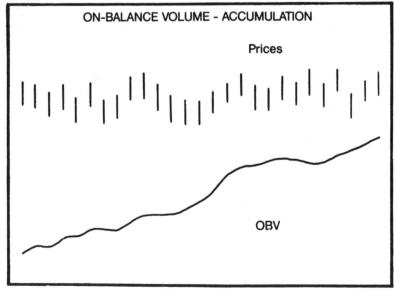

Figure 14-1

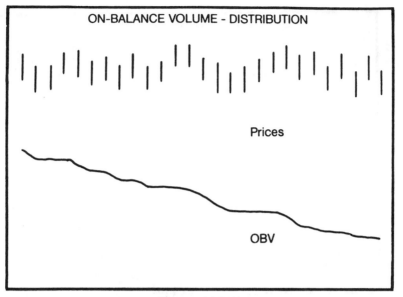

**Figure 14-2**

Distribution is indicated if prices are moving sideways and the OBV is falling. We could conclude a major top is forming and prices should drop quickly. (Figure 14-2).

What if prices, instead of moving sideways, are in an uptrend while the OBV is moving sideways? Again, we would have a *divergence* between price and OBV. This divergence would indicate that the price rise is not being accompanied by strong volume and that this market is weak and could easily reverse (Figure 14-3).

Some analysts feel that this method for calculating the basic OBV may be too simplistic. Since each day's price change is determined by transactions on *both* the buying and selling side, they feel it is an exaggeration to assign *all* the volume to the plus or minus side simply because the close one day is higher or lower than the close of the preceding day. Others argue that a more reasonable approach would be to ignore the previous day's close and determine if prices rise or fall from today's open to today's close.

**MARK CHAIKEN'S VOLUME ACCUMULATOR** is an alternative to the Granville On-Balance Volume System which is supposed to

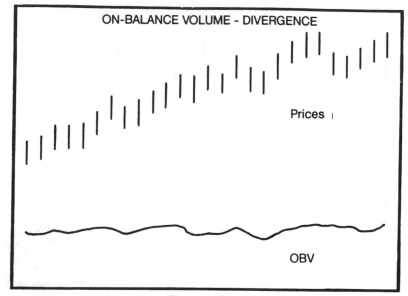

**Figure 14-3**

solve this problem. It provides a more sensitive intraday measurement of volume in relation to price action. He does this by placing added emphasis upon the day's close in relation to its average or *mean* price for that day. For example, if the close is above the mean, a percentage of the volume is assigned a positive value. Conversely, if it falls below the mean, a portion is considered negative. If the close is the same as the high, all volume is treated as positive. Likewise, if the close is the same as the low, all volume is treated as negative.

A cumulative line is drawn and, like in Granville's OBV, the trader is advised to look for divergences between this line and the price trend. For example, if the cumulative line fails to confirm an upward trend, a decline in price may be indicated.

Although the Volume Accumulator and Granville's OBV will often agree, this is not always the case. Comparing Figure 14-4, you will notice the difference in these two indicators when applied to the same data.

Still, with all its faults, OBV is a very useful tool for spotting accumulation and distribution. For a much more comprehensive study of OBV, traders can refer to Granville's *New Strategy of Daily Stock Market Trading for Maximum Profit.*

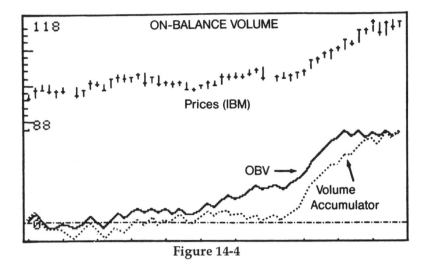

**Figure 14-4**

With the array of tools you have mastered regarding price and volume analysis, you have now taken the first important steps toward your goal of consistently winning in the markets. Most of the techniques you have learned can be applied equally well to any market—individual stocks, the Dow Jones averages, gold, silver, soybeans, the German mark, T-bonds—you name it. But when you attempt to analyze the stock market you will need additional tools designed specifically for that purpose.

# PART III

## STOCK MARKET

# 15

# "THE AVERAGES" AND DOW THEORY

How is the stock market doing? Sounds like a simple question. But in fact it is an extremely provocative one—one which you will find more difficult to answer with a brief reply the more you learn about the market. Usually the person who poses the question wants to hear "good," "bad," or "indifferent." But for you and I who study the stock market, it's not that simple. A one-word answer tells us nothing about chart patterns, volume, divergences, nonconfirmations of the various averages, the various industry sectors, etc. It doesn't even address the fundamental problem: What is the stock market?

The stock market is really the sum total of *each and every* stock that is traded. The problem is we usually don't measure it that way. Instead we use a variety of market "averages" which reflect far more limited samples of stocks considered representative of the total.

**THE DOW JONES INDUSTRIAL AVERAGE** is the most popular and tracks the price of 30 large industrial companies, but was never intended by its inventor, Charles H. Dow, to be analyzed or tracked to the exclusion of the other Dow Jones averages—20 transportations, 15 utilities and 65 composite stocks. Nevertheless, it is the Industrials which are the most widely followed of the four and the one usually referred to in summaries of daily stock-market activity.

The broader market averages—the Standard and Poor's 500 Stock

Index (S&P 500), the New York Stock Exchange Index (NYSE), and sometimes the Value Line Index—are often preferred by market professionals and technical analysts because they are more representative of the overall market than the 30 Dow Jones Industrials.

**THE S&P INDEX** represents 500 heavily capitalized, blue chip companies.

**THE NEW YORK STOCK EXCHANGE INDEX**, created in 1966 as a result of criticism that the Dow is not a true reflector of the market, comprises *all* stocks listed on the New York Stock Exchange and is thus the broadest measure of that market.

**THE VALUE LINE**, is comprised of 1,700 stocks listed on various exchanges and is unique in that it is the only "unweighted" average of those discussed here. This means that each stock, regardless of its price, is weighted equally in determining the index value. Thus, by watching this index in relationship to the S&P, for example, you can judge how the secondary, less capitalized companies are doing in relation to the "blue chips."

Dow Theory is not a fancy little formula for which you can buy software. Instead, it is a comprehensive "theory" of stock market behavior. It is, in effect, one of the first major "technical" studies ever attempted on the stock market, and though occasionally criticized, still must be considered to be a valuable tool due to its long record of success in stock-market prognostication.

In 1897, two market averages were compiled. The "Rails," which included 20 railroad companies, have since been broadened to include the airlines and renamed the "Transports." The Industrial Average, representing most other types of business and made up originally of only 12 issues, was increased later to 20 in 1916 and 30 in 1928. In 1929, all stocks of public utility companies were dropped from the Industrial Average and a new Utility Average of 20 issues was set up, and reduced to 15 in 1936. Finally, the three have been averaged together to make the Dow Jones 65 - Stock Composite Index. Traditional Dow Theory pays no attention to the utility or composite averages; its interpretations are based exclusively on the Rails (transports) and Industrials.

There is much to suggest that Charles H. Dow did not think of his theory as a device for forecasting the stock market, but rather as a barometer of general business trends. The basic principles of the theory were outlined by him in editorials he wrote for the *Wall Street Journal.* Upon his death in 1902, his successor as editor of the newspaper, William P. Hamilton, took up Dow's principles and, in the course of 27 years of writing on the market, formulated them into the Dow Theory as we know it today. As you read the basic tenets of the Dow Theory below, you will soon see the origin of basic terminology and theory used in modern-day technical analysis.

1.   **THE AVERAGES DISCOUNT EVERYTHING THAT CAN BE KNOWN.** Because the averages reflect the combined market activities of thousands of investors, including those possessing the best foresight and information, the averages in their day-to-day fluctuations discount everything known, everything foreseeable, and every condition which can affect the supply or demand for stocks. Unpredictable happenings such as earthquakes may not be reflected in the averages, but they are soon appraised after they occur. Because of this discounting function, the behavior of the averages affords the first clue as to the future of stock prices.

2.   **THE THREE TRENDS.** The three trends that are continually unfolding are the Primary (Major Trend), Secondary (Intermediate Trend), and Day-to-Day (Minor Trend). These trends are sometimes likened to the ocean's tide, waves and ripples.

3.   **THE PRIMARY TRENDS.** These broad movements usually last for more than a year and may run for several years, resulting in general appreciation or depreciation in value of more than 20 percent. So long as each successive rally reaches a higher level than the one before it and each secondary reaction stops at a higher level than the previous reaction, the Primary Trend is up and we are in a *bull market.* Conversely, when each intermediate

decline carries prices to successively lower levels and each inter-vening rally fails to exceed the top of the previous rally, the Primary Trend is down and we are in a *bear market.*

4.    **THE SECONDARY TRENDS** are reactions occurring in a bull market and *rallies* occurring in a bear market. Normally, they last from a few weeks to a few months and retrace from one-third to two-thirds of the gain or loss registered by the preceding swing in the Primary Trend.

5.    **THE MINOR TRENDS.** The Secondary Trend is composed of Minor Trends or day-to-day fluctuations which are considered unimportant to the Dow theorist. They usually last less than six days but may last up to three weeks.

6.    **THE BULL MARKET.** The Primary Trend usually consists of three phases. The first phase is known as "accumulation" and occurs when business conditions are still poor and the public is generally discouraged with the stock market. The second phase is usually a fairly steady advance on increasing activity as busi-ness conditions and corporate earnings begin to improve. The third phase is characterized by highly publicized "good news." Price gains are often spectacular and the public becomes heavily involved.

7.    **THE BEAR MARKET.** Primary down trends are also usually characterized by three phases. The first phase, known as distribu-tion, is when farsighted investors sell their shares to the less informed public. The second phase is the panic phase. In this phase buying decreases, selling becomes more urgent, and the downward trend of prices accelerates on mounting volume. After the panic phase, there may be a fairly long secondary recovery or a sidewise movement. Finally, the business news begins to dete-riorate and prices resume their decline though less rapidly than before. The bear market ends when everything possible in the way of bad news has been discounted.

8. **PRINCIPLE OF CONFIRMATION.** No valid signals of a change in trend can be generated by either the industrials or rails (transports) independent of the other. In other words, if one average makes a new high over its previous peak but the other average falls short of exceeding its previous peak, a nonconfirmation has occurred. The move must be considered suspect until both averages confirm by exceeding their previous peaks.

9. **VOLUME.** In bull markets volume tends to increase on rallies and decrease on declines. But, in Dow Theory, *conclusive* signals as to the market's trend can only be produced by price movement. Volume only affords collateral evidence which may aid interpretation of otherwise doubtful situations.

10. **LINES.** A Line refers to a sidewise movement in one or both of the averages, which lasts from a few weeks to a few months, in the course of which price fluctuates within a range of approximately 5 percent. A Line can substitute for a Secondary Trend. A breakout from the Line area is usually significant. It cannot be known in advance which way the breakout will occur, but more often than not, it is in the direction of the trend.

11. **CLOSING PRICES.** Dow Theory pays no attention to any extreme highs or lows which may be registered intraday, but takes into account only the closing figures.

12. **A TREND IN EFFECT CONTINUES UNTIL REVERSED.** This final tenet simply means that once a new primary trend is definitely signaled by the action of the two averages, the odds that it will continue, despite any near-term reactions, are at their greatest. But as the Primary Trend carries on, the odds in favor of its further extension grow smaller.

# 16

# BREADTH OF MARKET INDICATORS

THE ADVANCE-DECLINE LINE is the most common measure of market breadth and is considered to be one of the most important technical indicators of the condition of the stock market. It is derived by taking the difference between the number of advancing issues and the number of declining issues each day. This daily figure is then added or subtracted each day to a cumulative number in order to determine the advance-decline line.

The purpose is to tell you if the market *as a whole* is gaining strength or losing strength—a measure which will often signal a major change in the direction of the market before any of the averages. As an example, when the Dow is advancing, yet the advance-decline line is falling, it means that even though the Dow is up, a majority of the *other* stocks is declining—a warning that the "technical condition" of the market is deteriorating and that the bull market is in "poor health."

Conversely, if the Dow is falling, yet the advance-decline line is rising, it implies that even though the Dow stocks are declining, a majority of other stocks are beginning to advance—a good signal that the market is technically strong and may turn upward shortly.

The theory behind the advance-decline line can best be understood by the "bathtub" analogy. Picture the market as a bathtub and the water level as represented by the advance-decline line. Advancing stocks raise the water level and declining stocks lower the water level. Market strength or weakness is determined by that water level.

The "smart money" is always the first to get out when the water level of the market stops rising and starts to come down, even though the Dow may still be an uptrend. This smart money is the first "water" to flow out the drain. Likewise, the "dumb money" is the last water to leave the tub — when the flow is speeded up, panic selling takes place and the lowest prices are reached in one last precipitous drop.

At that time, the bear market has ended and a new bull market is about to begin. Just as the smart money was the first to leave the bathtub when it was full, it is also the smart money which will be the first to flow back when it is empty.

The smart money then becomes the bottom layer of water, the foundation upon which the new bull market will be built, and on which all the other layers of water will rest. Thus, smart money is the first in and first out; while dumb money, sitting up on the surface, is last in, last out.

Simply enough so far. But a little more study reveals that we must also consider *which phase* of the bull or bear market we are in and whether we are attempting to predict a market top or market bottom.

The first phase of a bull market is characterized by a rising advance-decline line as the smart money enters the market.

In the second phase, the advance-decline line also trends higher but usually tops out late in the second phase or early in the third phase as the smart money begins to get out.

In the third phase, it should clearly complete its rise, signalling the end of the bull market. The advance-decline line then trends lower throughout the first two phases of the near bear market and most, if not all, of the third phase.

I find that the advance-decline line indicator is much better at picking market tops than market bottoms. Market tops are always forewarned by a declining advance-decline line. During bear market bottoms, however, the advance-decline line often turns up at the same time as the Dow and sometimes even later with a certain lag. Notice in Figure 16-1 how the advance-decline line gave no warning that the market was about to bottom in August 1982.

Here's a recap of the possible advance/decline situations. (Remember to take into consideration what phase the market appears to be in. Also, never rely solely on one indicator alone.)

### TABLE 16-1. ADVANCE/DECLINE INDICATOR

| Dow | Advance/Decline Line | Prognosis |
|---|---|---|
| Rising prices | Falling | Lower |
| Approaching or at previous top | Considerably below corresponding top | Lower prices |
| Approaching or at previous top | Considerably above corresponding top | Still higher prices |
| Falling | Rising* | Higher prices |
| Approaching or at previous bottom | Considerably above previous bottom | Higher prices |
| Approaching or at previous bottom | Considerably below previous bottom | Still lower prices |

*Time lag possible here. Should be used more as a confirming than a forecasting tool.*

The advance-decline line in its "raw" form is shown in Figure 16-1. It is simply a cumulative sum of advances minus declines.

Some analysts prefer the smoothing effects of a moving average, with a 10-day moving average commonly used (see Figure 16-2).

**THE UNCHANGED ISSUES INDEX** is also a valuable tool. Sometimes it is useful to watch not only the numbers of stocks that advance and decline but also the number that remain unchanged. In theory, when a higher than normal percentage of stocks remain unchanged in price, the market is likely making a top. The index is calculated each day by dividing the number of issues which are unchanged in price by the total number of stocks traded. The percentage derived from the calculation will usually fluctuate in a range between 5 percent and 25 percent. Readings near the low end of the

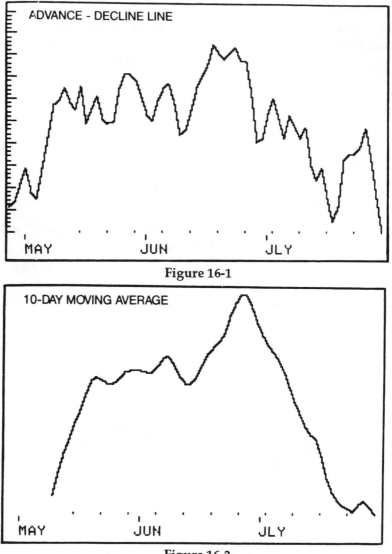

**Figure 16-1**

**Figure 16-2**

range are considered bullish, while readings near the high end are bearish.

## Advanced Indicators

Over the years, many analysts have developed sophisticated breadth indices by *combining* volume with advance-decline data. The remainder of this chapter explores eight unique market breadth indices, each developed by a different analyst. The material is quite technical and is included here as a reference for those who might want to explore the concept of market breadth more deeply. Others may wish to skip to the next chapter.

**THE HAURLAN INDEX** developed by Dave Holt, publisher of *Trade Levels,* takes the advance/decline concept one step further. This index is made up of three different moving averages which flash short-term, intermediate, and long-term buy or sell signals.

In the Haurlan Index, the short-term index is a 3-day weighted moving average of advances over declines. When the index moves above +100, a short-term buy signal is generated, which remains in effect until the index drops below –150 at which time a sell signal is generated. The sell signal then remains in effect until the index moves above +100 again and so on:

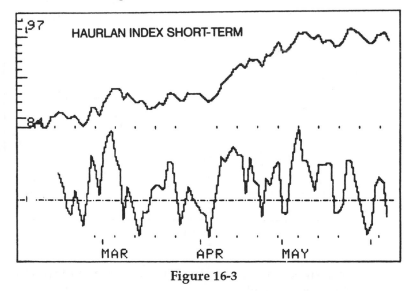

**Figure 16-3**

The Haurlan Intermediate Term Index is a 20-day weighted moving average, interpreted the same way you would interpret any price chart.

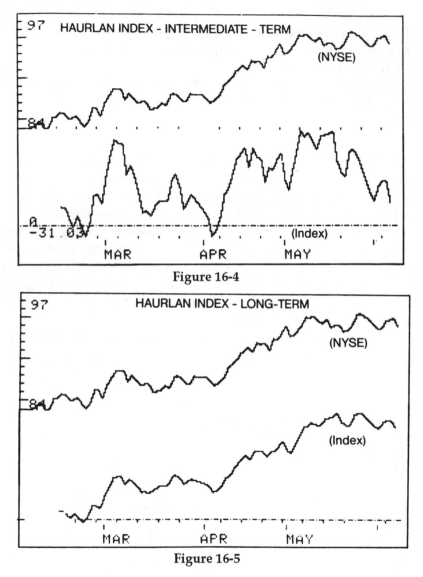

**Figure 16-4**

**Figure 16-5**

Buy and sell signals are determined by the crossing of trend lines or support/resistance levels.

The Long-term Index—a 200-day weighted moving average of net advances over declines—is used to measure the primary trend of the market and not to determine precisely timed buy and sell points.

**THE McCLELLAN OSCILLATOR and SUMMATION INDEX** developed in the late '60s by Sherman and Marian McClellan, rep-

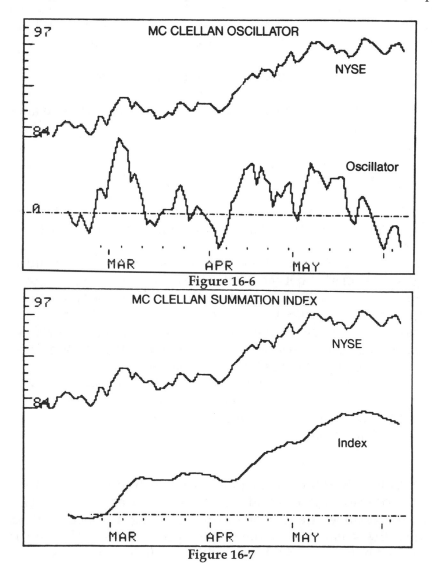

Figure 16-6

Figure 16-7

resent another approach to the advance/decline concept. They are a short- to intermediate-term indicator of market behavior, pointing out overbought and oversold conditions. They use the same advance-decline line, but take the difference between the equivalent of a weighted 20-day moving average and a weighted 40-day moving average. This then behaves like an oscillator, fluctuating between a maximum and minimum range, forming chart patterns which are useful in forecasting market turns and the duration of market moves.

The McClellan Oscillator has two important characteristics:

1.    The oscillator then passes through zero at or very soon after the turning points.

2.    The oscillator then passes through zero at or very soon *after* the turning points.

The Summation Index—a cumulative total of each day's McClellan Oscillator value—has the ability to forecast the longer term trend of the market (Figure 16-7).

Figure 16-8 shows the position of the Summation Index at the August 1982 market bottom. Notice how it failed to go lower than in June. It is especially important to study this time period because it represented a market turning point that ushered in one of the greatest bull markets of the century. This indicator boldly forewarned those with a technical ear to the market that the long bear market was over and it was time to buy stocks.

A 50-page booklet, *Patterns for Profit,* detailing how to use and interpret both the McClellan Oscillator and Summation Index is available from Trade Levels, Inc., 21241 Ventura Boulevard, Suite 269, Woodland Hills, CA 91364.

**THE ARMS INDEX** is among those that take the breadth of market studies one step further by adding *volume* to the equation. It measures the relative strength of volume entering advancing stocks against the strength of volume entering declining stocks, and is calculated as follows: Divide the number of advancing stocks by the

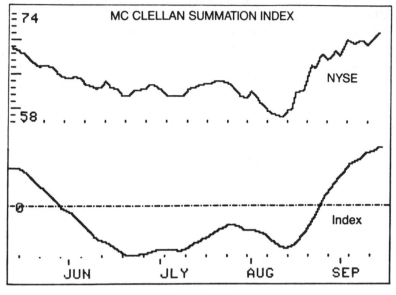

**Figure 16-8**

number of declining stocks. Then divide the upside volume by the downside volume. Finally, divide the first answer by the second result. Expressed in a formula:

$$X = (A/D) / (UV/DV)$$
where X = Arms Index
A = advancing stocks
D = declining stocks
UV = upside volume
DV = downside volume

This gives you the short-term index. Readings below 1.0 are bullish; readings above 1.0 are bearish. Extreme readings of 1.50 or higher are very bearish; and of .50 or lower very bullish. "Climax readings" would be at 2.00 and .30.

A short- to medium-term trading signal can be obtained by plotting a 5-day moving average of the short-term index. Here, a sell signal is generated when the index rises above 1.00; a buy signal produced when it falls below 1.00.

An intermediate to long-term trading signal can be generated by using a 10-day moving average of the index and, as such, it may be

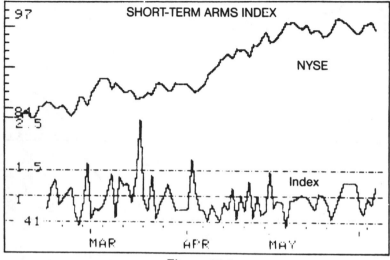

**Figure 16-9**

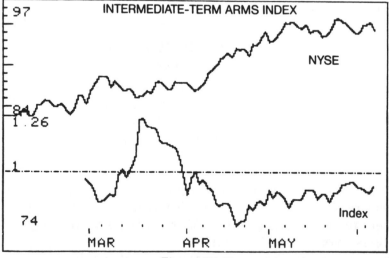

**Figure 16-10**

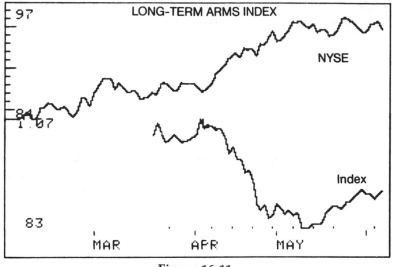

**Figure 16-11**

viewed as an overbought/oversold indicator. A longer term signal can be produced by using a 10-day/25-day moving average cross-over of the index. On the resulting graphs (see Figures 16-9, 16-10 and 16-11) you can also use trendline and support/resistance theory. (More information on this system can be found in Gerald Appel's *Winning Stock Selection Systems*, published by Signalert Corporation, Great Neck, New York.)

**THE HUGHES BREADTH INDICATOR** is the result of some of the most exhaustive work on market breadth conducted by James F. Hughes. He used an advance-decline ratio which is derived by subtracting the number of declines from the number of advances and the dividing that number by the total issues traded. The following conclusions were abstracted from his *Weekly Market Letter*, written from 1960 to 1964 while at the New York firm of Auchincloss, Parker and Redpath.

Hughes believed that sustained major advances in the market are completely dependent upon a harmonious relationship between breadth and price. Indeed, he found good reason to be concerned whenever the breadth index began to decline while the Dow Jones

Averages continued to advance. His research showed that all major declines since 1919 were preceded by three to ten weeks of a declining trend in the breadth index, during which period the DJIA could stage at least two rallies to new highs without confirmation by the indicator. Following such as divergence, the DJIA would generally decline to levels *below* the price level it had reached at the time the breadth index reached *its* high.

Such major divergences do not generally occur in markets which are in trading ranges. Rather, they are associated with periods of high speculative activity following sustained advances. Therefore, although relatively rare, when they do occur, major breadth/price divergences carry with them a high technical probability that the subsequent decline will end with a multiple price collapse or "selling climax."

**A SELLING CLIMAX** occurs under the following circumstances:

(a)   Daily declines should represent 70 percent or more of total issues traded and daily advances 15 percent or less of total issues traded.

(b)   Until the market has a day or two of visible technical recovery, consecutive climax days are counted as only *one* selling climax.

(c)   Following one selling climax, if a rally fails to gain 50 percent of the ground lost during the decline, the decline should resume. If a second climax appears, the rally objective is raised to two-thirds of the decline. And, following a triple selling climax, technical probabilities highly favor a 20 percent rally from the lows. Until you have an indication of at least three selling climaxes, there is no justification for buying. But, as a general rule, whenever five temporary selling climaxes are crowded into thirty-five days or less, the investor can purchase stocks for a move up of intermediate proportions.

As we saw earlier in the chapter, the failure of our breadth indicators to confirm a new high in the Dow implied lower prices.

But it does not necessarily mean that a *major* decline is imminent. Such nonconfirmation has frequently preceded relatively *minor* intermediate trading swings. However, it can be very helpful because as long as the breadth is continuing to make new highs, even if the Dow is not, a bear market is highly unlikely; and, any reaction which develops without a divergence must be regarded as only an intermediate interruption of an uptrend, (this is supported by documentation which goes back as far as 1934).

**A BUYING CLIMAX**, although not defined by Hughes, can be characterized with criteria which are similar to those of the selling climax: Advancing issues representing 70 percent or more of total issues and declining issues 15 percent or less. Since a buying climax takes place generally near intermediate bottoms—not the ultimate tops—and is often followed by new highs, its significance is not as great as a selling climax.

We have programmed our computer to look for selling climaxes and find it to be quite accurate in spotting short-term oversold conditions that are likely to result in a bounceback the next day (Figure 16-12).

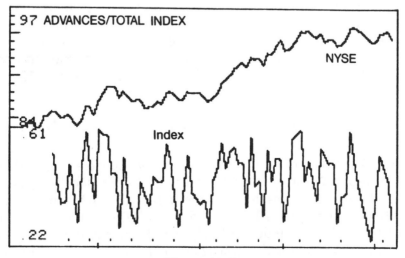

**Figure 16-12**

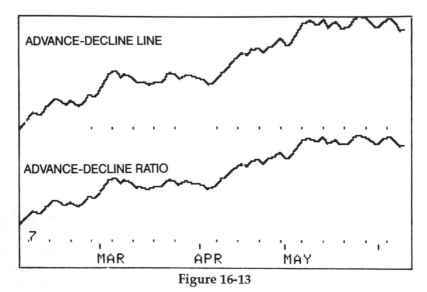

**Figure 16-13**

**RICHARD RUSSELL**, publisher of *Dow Theory Letters*, is well known for his work on breadth. Like Hughes, he also uses the advance/decline ratio which he computes by subtracting the number of declining issues and dividing the result by the total issues traded (A - D)/T. Like Hughes, Russell rates this indicator highly, writing that: "In general, I have found the AD ratio to be the dominant indicator or the more reliable indicator of the primary trend of the market. Thus highs on breadth unconfirmed by highs on the Industrial Average generally occur only within a primary bull market. Conversely, new lows on the Industrial Average generally occur within the framework of primary bear markets" (Figure 16-13).

The **A/D LINE** is not significantly different from the A/D RATIO.

**PAUL DYSART**, editor of *Trendway Economic Services*, uses the basic advance-decline line which he calls his Composite Basic Issues Traded Index. He takes this idea one step further in his creation of a Positive Volume Issues Traded Index (PVITI) and a Negative Volume Issues Traded Index (NVITI). The former is the summation minus declines *only on days when total volume of trading increases over that of the previous day*. The latter is defined similarly on days when

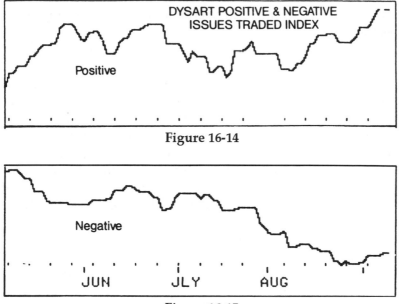

**Figure 16-14**

**Figure 16-15**

volume of trading *decreased* from the previous day, and it is this one which Dysart feels is the most valuable since it measures the way the market regains its equilibrium after the effect of increased volume days.

**HAMILTON BOLTON,** the late editor of the *Bolton-Tremblay Bank Credit Analyst,* was one of the few analysts who calculated an advance-decline index using the *unchanged* issues as a basic component. He used the square root of the difference between the ratio of advances to unchanged and the ratio of declining to unchanged (**BOLTON INDEX** = square root of A/U - D/U). His reasons for the square root was that it eliminated a strong downward bias.

In dynamic up and down phases of the market, Bolton's index is impacted by (1) heavy excesses of advances over declines or vice versa, and (2) a shrinking, unchanged component in the denominator. In top areas, however, and in slow bottom areas, unchanged issues tend to expand, reducing the index. Such action helps indicate a turn in trend and supports the contention of underlying strength or weakness.

**WALTER HEIBY,** in his exhaustive book on market breadth, *Stock Market Profits Through Dynamic Synthesis,* concludes that the usual breadth-of-market studies are not complete and do not always hold true. He points to the 1963-64 period when the number of advancing issues each day was a continual disappointment, leading many analysts to expect a major decline which never materialized; and he suggests that the breadth indicators in those years reflected high institutional demand for Dow Jones quality stocks. The fact that the public refused to make the advance a broader one should not have swayed the investor from a bullish posture. Heiby's point has become particularly relevant in today's environment of uncertainty and with institutions accounting for an increasingly larger percentage of stock market trading.

Heiby's answer, which he calls the "Dynamic Synthesis," essentially involves the following steps: First, he takes the last 50-day trading period and splits the chart into four horizontal quartiles—top, bottom, and two in the middle. Second, he looks for four criteria which must be met to obtain a valid buy signal which he calls the "Advance-Decline Quartile Divergence Syndrome."

To obtain a buy signal, four criteria must be met:

1.    The Standard and Poor's Composite Index must be in the bottom quartile.

2.    The Advancing Issues Index must be in the top quartile.

3.    The Advancing Issues Index must be greater than the Declining Issues Index.

4.    The Unchanged Issues must not be in the top quartile.

Similarly, to obtain a sell signal, five criteria must be met:

1.    The Standard and Poor's Composite Index must be in the top quartile.

2.    The Advancing Issues Index must be in the bottom quartile.

3.    The Declining Issues Index must be in the top quartile.

4.    The Advancing Issues Index must be less than the Declining Issues Index.

5.    The Unchanged Issues Index must not be in the lowest quartile.

Finally, after one or another of these sets of criteria have been met, he looks at other indicators such as short sales, odd-lot sales, and odd-lot purchase volume.

# 17

# LEADERSHIP AND QUALITY

During a stock-market rise, determining the quality of stocks leading the advance often can lend an important clue as to what phase it is in. In general, bull markets begin with the high quality blue chips. Then, after a correction, somewhat lower priced stocks are thought to be bargains and rapidly gain investor attention. By the third and final phase of the market advance, the cheaper, more speculative issues—often found on the over-the-counter market or the American Exchange—now make the most rapid gains. This is usually an indication that the bull market is nearing its end.

**THE MOST ACTIVE ISSUES** is one of the best ways to monitor market leadership. The 15 Most Active Issues (published daily) and the 20 Most Active Issues (published weekly) list which stocks are being most actively bought and sold according to the number of shares traded. Therefore, the lists generally reflect the concentration of big money flows.

How do we determine a quality stock? Price is the best measure; and for the purpose of analysis, we can arbitrarily set the $40 mark as the key threshold: If the majority of the Most Actives has a price of greater than $40 per share, we would consider the advance to be led by *quality* stocks. On the other hand, if the majority of the Most

117

Actives are below $40 per share, with some in the $10-25 price range, we would consider the advance to be primarily speculative, leading us to expect a possible stock-market decline.

When attempting to catch short-term swings, you plot the percentage of the 15 Most Actives that showed a gain for that day. As an example, if 10 issues rise, 2 decline and 3 issues remain unchanged, you would plot 10/15 or 67 percent. Then you take a 10-day moving average of those percentages.

When the indicator reaches the 60-70 percent region and starts to turn down, the market will usually be overbought and due for at least a short-term correction. However, if the indicator exceeds 70 percent, an entirely different signal is flashed and a powerful advance can be expected.

Likewise, when the indicator descends to 30-35 percent and begins to turn up, the market will be oversold and due for at least a short-term rally. During bear markets, readings of 30 percent are more usual (Figure 17-1).

Generally we find that divergences between the trend of the indicator and the trend of the market can also be used to help call turning points. If the indicator is rising while prices are falling, expect the market to turn up. Conversely, if the indicator is falling while the market is rising, expect the market to turn down.

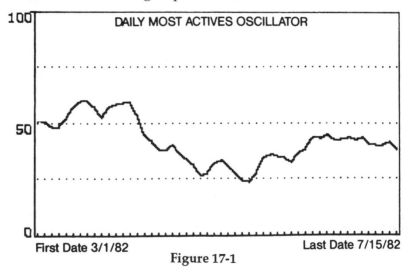

**Figure 17-1**

Another shorter term indicator using the 15 Most Active Issues is employed by *Indicator Digest* (451 Grand Ave., Palisades Park, NJ 07650). To compute the indicator, simply subtract declining issues from advancing issues. For example, if 10 rose, 4 declined and 1 remained unchanged, the net for the day is 6. If 5 rose, 8 declined and 2 remained unchanged, the net would be -3.

Maintain a 30-day cumulative total of the latest 30 days' reading. As illustrated in Figure 17-2, a buy signal is generated when the 30-day total rises to +9; a sell signal is generated when the 30-day total falls to below -9; and readings between +9 and -9 are neutral, meaning that the previous signal remains in effect.

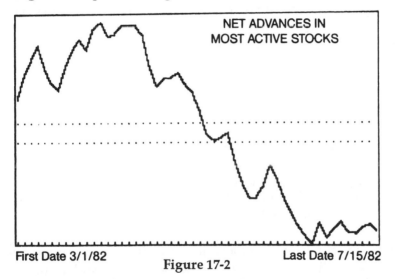

NET ADVANCES IN
MOST ACTIVE STOCKS

**First Date 3/1/82**        **Last Date 7/15/82**

**Figure 17-2**

**NEW HIGHS AND NEW LOWS.** This indicator, like the advance-decline line, is also a breadth-of-the-market indicator and can be used in much the same way. "New highs" are defined as the number of issues that have made new highs during the latest 52-week period; whereas "new lows" designate the number of issues that have made new lows during that period.

For instance, if the number of new highs is expanding, it can be considered a bullish sign. If the number of new highs is contracting, while the number of new lows is expanding, it may be considered bearish. The problem is that this interpretation is a bit oversimplified; you really must also consider other factors or it can lead you astray. You must be aware of what phase the market is in and whether divergence exists between your high/low indicator and the market itself.

Let's assume that the Dow Jones has been entrenched in a bear market for two years and your indicator is showing zero stocks at new highs and 650 stocks at new lows. A month later the Dow Jones has plummeted another 50 points, but now the indicator shows 5 stocks at new highs and only 500 stocks at new lows. This is exactly what we are looking for—a major nonconfirmation. It means that 150 stocks have rallied from their lows—an extremely significant event, signalling the end of the bear market. But the context in which all this has occurred is the key. Since the bear market has been in force for two years and since the entire stock-market cycle is typically four to four and a half years, we are overdue for a turnaround. If the bear market had recently begun, we would not attach much significance to a similar pattern. Figure 17-3 shows the pattern of new highs and new lows during the critical summer of 1982 prior to the record-smashing rally which soon ensued.

Now, assume a new bull market has begun. At first, the new lows still outnumber the new highs. But we are concerned only with the trend—the fact that each day there are *more* new highs and *fewer* new lows. After four months, the Dow Jones has risen 150 points and our high/low indicator looks healthy. We now have 550 new highs and zero new lows.

One month later, the Dow Jones is 50 points higher but the high/low indicator shows only 400 new highs and 10 new lows. Should we be concerned? Is this the end of the bull market? Maybe not. If, in fact, we are correct in identifying the last major bottom and we are truly in a new bull market, it could be too early for it to be terminating. Rather than a new bear market, our high/low indicator is probably signalling a correction.

It is normal after the first major advance in a bull market for the number of new highs to decrease somewhat—usually as the Dow Jones is entering its first corrective phase. However, if the Dow continues to advance despite a declining number of new highs, it often indicates that a more severe correction is in the making.

To complete the cycle, assume we are two to two and a half years

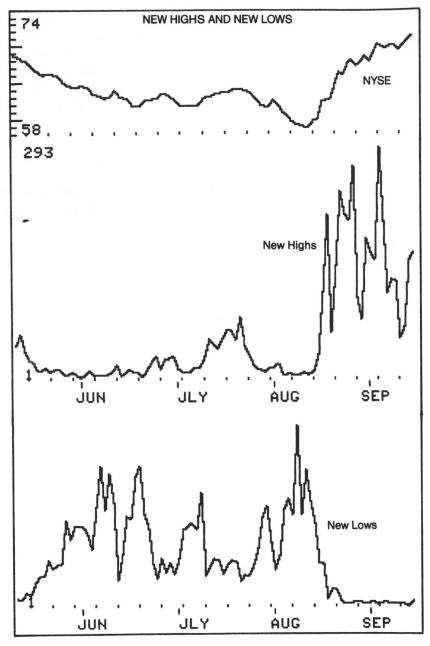

Figure 17-3

into the bull market. We're on the lookout for a turnaround and we detect a serious divergence between the Dow Jones and the high/low indicator: The Dow Jones is still moving higher while the number of new highs is declining. This time, the nonconfirmation can be taken more seriously. Although the peaking out of the number of new highs usually occurs months in advance of the final high in the Dow, this is a good time to begin an orderly liquidation process.

Thus, the high/low indicator can be a valuable tool—*if used properly and in conjunction with other indicators.*

We now move to an area which we consider to be among the most important if you are going to properly time the markets, namely **market sentiment.**

# 18

# MARKET SENTIMENT INDICATORS

Market sentiment indicators are those which attempt to gauge the mood of market participants—generally classified as either "sophisticated" or "unsophisticated."

Sophisticated market players are professionals who make their living from stock-market trading. The specialists, for example, concentrate on only one or two issues and trade on the floor of the Exchange for their own account. In order to give each stock better liquidity and to make a more orderly market for the general public, they are required to buy in the absence of other competing bids and to sell in the absence of other competing offers.

Another group, the Exchange members, are those who have purchased a "seat" on the Exchange. This allows them to trade on the floor without paying commissions.

Although there are, of course, many notable exceptions, as a whole the general public is most often thought to be unsophisticated and, more often than not, wrong in the world of stock-market trading. Therefore, their activity is also watched very closely for a clue as to where the market may be headed.

Professionals consider market sentiment indicators to be among their most valuable tools. The indicators in this chapter will enable you to determine the "mood" of each of the three groups of market participants discussed.

The **SHORT INTEREST RATIO,** published monthly in *Barron's* is designed to spot when the public becomes overly pessimistic. It is calculated by dividing the total number of short sales outstanding on the NYSE by the average daily trading volume on the exchange that month. If the short interest ratio is above 1.75, it is considered a bullish signal. A reading of slightly above 2.0 (a short interest of twice the average daily volume) was recorded in June of 1982, two months ahead of the dynamic rally that followed in August. Another time the ratio had reached 2.0 was in July 1970, also a very good time to buy stocks.

On the opposite side of the spectrum, the indicator has, on occasion, been used to signal excessive public optimism when the ratio has dropped below 1.0. But such bearish signals have turned out to be very unreliable on several occasions. Therefore *I suggest you use the short interest ratio primarily as a buy signal.*

**ODD-LOT PURCHASES OR SHORT SALES** refer to all transactions that involve less than 100 shares of stock. Since these purchases and sales are usually transacted by the less sophisticated market players, these figures, published daily in most newspapers, can often play a role in market timing.

It is not too difficult to compute this ratio. You can do so by dividing odd-lot short sales by total short sales each week. A moving average may then be used to smooth the data.

The basic theory is that a trend toward increased odd-lot selling is bullish; a trend toward decreased odd-lot selling is bearish. You may also look at the other side of the coin. A trend toward increased odd-lot buying is bearish; a trend toward decreased odd-lot buying is bullish.

It has been found that odd-lots often tend to panic and sell at the wrong times, with odd-lot short selling reaching a peak just as the market bottoms and still a second peak often reached as the market retests its bottom.

**SPECIALIST SHORT SALES**—by members of the New York Stock Exchange—is a good indicator of the "smart money movements." Since the specialist's purpose is to make an orderly market, he is restricted in trading activity by certain rules. Still, he is considered to be one of the most astute traders in the game, a fact which can be well documented by past performance. Therefore, when heavy specialist short selling is evident, it is usually a good time to be bearish on the market. Conversely, when specialist short selling is light, it often is a good time to be buying stocks. This is not to say that specialists are always right. But, should you notice that specialist short selling is decreasing at the same time as odd-lot short selling is increasing, one indicator is confirming the other, adding credence to the signal.

The Specialist Short Sale Ratio may be computed weekly by dividing the total number of short sales on the NYSE each week into the number of shares sold short by specialists in each week. These data can also be found in *Barron's*, but there is a two week time lag before the figures are released to the public.

*A buy signal* can be generated by a single weekly reading below 33 percent, or a series of four weekly readings averaging below 35 percent. *A sell signal* is indicated when a single weekly reading exceeds 58 percent or the average of the latest four weekly readings exceeds 55 percent. As with the Short Interest Ratio, buy signals tend to be more accurate than sell signals.

**MEMBER SHORT SALES** also tends to be a good "smart money indicator." Low short selling on the part of the members is considered bullish; heavy short selling is considered bearish. These data are carried weekly and can also be found in *Barron's*.

The Member Short-Sale Ratio is calculated by dividing (a) the number of shares sold short by members of the NYSE by (b) the total number of shares sold short that week. (On other occasions, if you want to look at the other side of the coin, you can divide (a) the number of shares sold short by *non*-members of the exchange by (b) total. The result is the "Public Short-Sale Ratio" which, of course, is simply the reciprocal of the Member Short-Sale Ratio.)

It has been found that a reading below 65 percent in the Member

Short-Sale Ratio is usually an excellent buy signal for an intermediate or major move. A study showing this historical relationship was conducted by Norman G. Fosback, in *Stock Market Logic* (The Institute for Economic Research, 3471 N. Federal Highway, Ft. Lauderdale, FL 33306). Here are the results:

### TABLE 18-1. MEMBER SHORT SALES AND THREE-MONTH MARKET PERFORMANCE (1941-75)

| Member Short Sales (average of last ten weeks) | S&P 500 Index (3 months later) | Probability of Rising Prices |
|---|---|---|
| over 80% | -1.1% | 48% |
| 75-80% | +0.5% | 54% |
| 70-75% | +3.3% | 68% |
| 65-70% | +4.5% | 75% |
| 0-65% | +5.9% | 88% |
| 35-year average | +1.9% | 62% |

When the 10-week moving average of Member Short Sales was less than 65 percent, the market's average gain 3 months later was 5.9 percent; six months later it was 16.5 percent; and one year later, 24.39 percent. This indicator also tends to produce better buy signals than sell signals. However, a sale is indicated when the ratio approaches 88 percent.

**MEMBER TRADING**, another indicator of member activity, is derived by subtracting the number of shares sold by members of the NYSE from the number purchased. Net buying, designated by a rising line, carries bullish implications. Conversely, a falling line indicates the Members have been selling and should be viewed bearishly. These data are also available weekly in *Barron's*.

**ART MERRILL** (Merrill Analysis Inc., Box 228, Chappaqua, NY 10514) has shown that this indicator—using an exponential moving average rather than the raw data—is among the most significant of intermediate and major trend indicators we're aware of. Another approach would be to maintain an exponential moving average of the net weekly cumulative total of member purchases minus sales. You can then chart the difference between the latest week's readings and the exponential moving average you are maintaining. Your indicator will rise as member trading becomes more positive and falls when it turns negative.

**ADVISORY SENTIMENT** is often best used as an indicator of contrary opinion. It is common knowledge that stock-market investment advisors tend, for the most part, to be trend followers. They tend to turn bullish quite quickly after market prices start rising and to stay bullish during the bull market. Therefore, with some notable exceptions, they cannot be relied upon for calling a market top. Conversely, when the market has been declining, advisors tend to get overly pessimistic, often right at what turns out to be a major bottom. In sum, they seem to do very poorly at the beginning and end of a bear market.

The degree of advisors' optimism and pessimism can best be determined by the "Sentiment Index" which is maintained by *Investors Intelligence* (2 East Avenue, Larchmont, NY 10538). Abe Cohen—the publisher who tallies the percentage of advisory services that are bullish and bearish—has found that bear markets generally touch bottom when 60 percent or more of advisory services turn outright bearish; but in bull markets, widespread bullish sentiment does not necessarily end the rise.

**CUSTOMER'S MARGIN DEBT** refers to the amount of money owed to New York Stock Exchange member firms by customers who have borrowed money to finance their stock purchases. This figure, calculated on the last trading day of each month by the NYSE, is not released to the public until two or three weeks later. The figure can be found in *Barron's* or obtained directly by writing to the New York Stock Exchange, 11 Wall Street, New York, NY 10005.

Margin-account traders have traditionally been considered among the more sophisticated stock-market investors. Watching their borrowing patterns reveals when they are buying or selling stocks. When margin debt is rapidly expanding, it indicates that this group is buying heavily; when margin debt is decreasing, it can be reasoned that they are liquidating on balance.

The trend of Customer's Margin Debt has proven to be an excellent long-term market indicator. You can plot a line representing Customer's Margin Debt and also a line representing a 12-month moving average of the same. A buy signal is given when the current figure moves above the 12-month moving average. A sell signal is rendered when the current figure drops below the 12-month moving average. This particular timing method, developed by Norman Fosback, has proven to be an excellent indicator of bull and bear markets during the past 35 years. The important tops of 1956, 1959, 1961, 1966, 1968 and 1973 were all accompanied or preceded by turns in Customer's Margin Debt. Similarly, troughs established in 1957, 1960, 1962, 1966, 1970 and 1974 were accompanied by upturns in Customer's Margin Debt.

**FREE CREDIT BALANCES** refers to the cash left on account with New York Stock Exchange member brokerage firms. This series is also published monthly and can be obtained either from *Barron's* or directly from the New York Stock Exchange.

Unlike Margin Debt figures, Free Credit Balances usually reflect the activity of small, unsophisticated investors. The reasoning behind this is that only unsophisticated investors would allow their cash balances to lie idle at brokerage firms earning no interest.

Rising credit balances indicate that the small investors are selling stock and thus can be interpreted bullishly. Falling credit balances mean small investors are buying and should be interpreted bearishly.

As with Customer's Margin Debt, a useful technique is to plot the current series of Free Credit Balances against a twelve-month moving average. A buy signal is generated when the current series crosses above the 12-month moving average; a sell signal occurs when the current series crosses below the 12-month moving average.

**DOW JONES UTILITY AVERAGE**—Because of their sensitivity to interest rates, the utility stocks are often seen as a bellwether for the entire market. Utility stocks are more sensitive to interest rates than other stocks for two reasons: 1) utilities are heavy borrowers and thus their earnings are easily hurt by rising interest rates; and 2) utilities customarily pay a high dividend yield and are often purchased as a substitute for bonds. When interest rates rise, investors are likely to sell their utility stocks—purchased originally for their yield—and rush to higher yielding, short-term instruments such as T-bills. Thus, the Dow Jones Utility Average is often considered to be a leading indicator for the major trend of the stock market.

A useful technique is to plot the Dow Jones Utility Average overlayed with a 15-week moving average. When the current readings are above the 15-week moving average, the utility stocks can be classified as being in an uptrend and the stock market also should continue higher. When current readings drop below the 15-week moving average, a sell signal is in order.

Market sentiment indicators—like the others considered in this book—are almost exclusively concerned with technical factors which are internal to the market. In the next chapter, however, we give a few examples of how your computer can also track fundamental monetary indicators.

# 19

# MONETARY INDICATORS

**NET FREE RESERVES** are an important measure of liquidity in the banking system. They represent the excess cash that banks hold over and above their legal required reserves and borrowings from the Federal Reserve. When banks are flush with funds, the banking system is termed to be in a "net free reserves" position. Under such conditions the banks have the ability to finance business growth and economic expansion.

When net free reserves are negative, the banking system is termed to be in a "net borrowed reserves" position. This means that money is tight and that the necessary funds to fuel a business expansion are not present in the banking system. Such conditions often presage market declines. Conversely, a net free reserves position by the banking system is usually followed by a rising stock market. Even more reliability can be given to the forecast when free reserves are expanding.

**MONEY SUPPLY.** Another measure of liquidity is the money supply itself. The percent change of money supply growth is a good indicator of future stock-market movements. Specifically, the percent change in M-1 growth over a 13-week period has a lagged positive correlation with the Standard and Poor's 500 Index with the maximum effect of the money supply change being exhibited some four weeks into the future.

The **DISCOUNT RATE**, the rate which the Federal Reserve charges its member banks, can often have a dramatic impact on stocks. After a major decline in interest rates (such as the Fed funds rate or T-bill rates) has ended and a rise has begun, a discount-rate hike by the Fed gives the incipient rise in rates an official stamp of approval and can easily set off a major decline in stocks. Conversely, after interest rates have risen dramatically and have begun to decline somewhat, a cut in the discount rate by the Fed is, in effect, their way of telling the market that they intend to pump money into the economy and push rates down, triggering a major stock-market rally.

Thus, as a general rule, a cut in the discount rate can be viewed as bullish for the stock market and an increase in the rate would be considered a negative. The maximum impact on the stock market is generally three weeks after a discount rate change. After a very long interest-rate decline, however a discount-rate cut can often be viewed as a climactic move. This is especially true if the Fed is trying to artificially lower interest rates by cutting the discount rate well *below* the Federal funds rate—the rate at which banks borrow from each other. The reverse is true after a major rise. In either case, you should be on the lookout for a turnaround in interest rates and, subsequently, in stocks.

**FEDERAL FUNDS RATE** refers to the rate that banks charge one another for overnight loans and is the most reliable tool for anticipating discount-rate changes. Banks in general have two sources available for borrowing: (1) from the Federal Reserve at the discount rate and (2) from other banks at the "fed funds rate." As a rule, banks prefer to borrow in the overnight "fed funds" market. But when the fed funds rate moves substantially higher than the discount rate, it will generally encourage them to seek more money from the Fed. This can be accurately viewed as having negative connotations for the stock market in that a discount rate hike could be triggered when the Fed Funds rate rises above the discount rate by one percentage point (100 basis points) or more.

These monetary indicators and the various other technical tools described here should help you to determine the general direction of the markets over the medium-term. But in order to further fine-tune your timing, the short-term market indicators may also come in handy as you will see in the next chapter.

# 20

# SHORT-TERM MARKET INDICATORS

With market volatility greater than ever before and with greater leverage available than in most past periods, short-term indicators have become more important in order to give you advance warning of sudden turns.

The **SHORT-TERM TRADING INDEX**, also known as TRIN, evaluates buying and selling pressure. Specifically, it measures the amount of volume going into advancing stocks versus the amount of volume going into declining issues and TRIN can be monitored on a daily or intraday basis. The formula is:

$$\text{TRIN} = \frac{(\text{\# of advancing issues}/\text{\# of declining issues})}{(\text{upside volume}/\text{downside volume})}$$

As an example, assume that on one day on the New York Stock Exchange we have:

|  | Issues (number) | Volume (millions of shares) |
|---|---|---|
| Advancing | 800 | 50 |
| Declining | 600 | 25 |

The TRIN that day would be equal to:

$$\text{TRIN} = \frac{(800/600)}{(50/25)} = \frac{1.33}{2.0} = .67$$

In this case, buying pressure was stronger than selling pressure as comparatively more volume was going into advancing issues. It is generally accepted that a TRIN of between .65 and .90 is a bullish sign for the short term, while a reading of below .65 is considered *very* bullish. Readings of .90 to 1.10 are regarded as neutral, while TRIN above 1.10 carried bearish connotations.

TRIN can be very helpful in timing your purchases and sales, allowing you to get the very best possible executions of your trades. This can sometimes be crucial, especially when dealing in the options market. For example, if I am planning to sell and TRIN is bullish, I am likely to place my "ask" (sell order) slightly above the current "bid." On the other hand, if TRIN is bearish, I usually place my orders to sell immediately or "at the market" as it is unlikely I will receive a better price by waiting.

Still another way to use TRIN is as a short-term confirmation or non-confirmation of the market averages. In other words, if the market declines one day while TRIN is registering a bullish reading, the chances are that the market decline will not continue. Such divergence over two or three days can often forewarn of a market bottom. Confirmation, on the other hand, would be implied when the market moves up and the TRIN is bullish. In such a case, we would expect still higher prices—at least in the near term.

The Short-Term Trading Index is also sometimes employed as an overbought/oversold indicator by using its 10-day moving average (Figure 20-1).

If the 10-day moving average of TRIN is below .75, the market is considered to be overbought. If, in addition, the previous one-day reading exceeds 1.20, an immediate correction can be expected.

Conversely, if the 10-day moving average of TRIN is above 1.20, the market is considered to be oversold; and if, in addition, the previous one-day reading is below .65, an immediate corrective rally is called for.

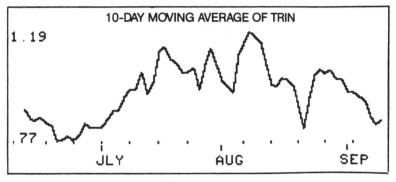

**Figure 20-1**

**THE TICK** indicator is another very commonly cited short-term barometer used intraday since it is updated every few minutes. It refers to the net upticks at that point in time, and can be best described as a snapshot taken of the market which "freezes" the action on the New York Stock Exchange. Each stock whose last trade is completed at a higher price than the previous trade is considered an "uptick." Each stock whose last trade is completed at a lower price is counted as a "downtick." The Tick indicator simply equals all upticks minus all downticks. If traders are bidding prices up, it will be recorded as a higher tick reading. Any reading above +100 is considered bullish, anything between -100 and +100 is neutral, and below -100 is bearish. Thus, the Tick is probably the most sensitive of all market indicators; and by watching *both* the Tick and TRIN you can develop a very good feel for the immediate market direction, timing your purchases and sales accordingly.

# 21

# INDUSTRY GROUPS

Most stocks can be classified according to groups—General Motors, Ford and Chrysler in the automobile group; ASA and HOMESTAKE in the goldmining group, etc. Since most companies within a group tend to move in unison, monitoring their performance can be helpful in various ways: By charting the performance of each group, you can quickly see which ones are leading an advance and which are lagging behind. If you intend to buy particular stocks, the information can make the selection process much easier. Needless to say, it is usually better to buy those issues which are members of an industry group which is leading the market move.

**RELATIVE STRENGTH** tracks industry groups in comparison to the market as a whole. The performance of each group is compared individually to the performance of the New York Stock Exchange Composite Index over a selected period of time, allowing you to analyze whether it is outperforming or underperforming the general market. A ranking can then be assigned to each industry group in terms of its relative strength.

I have developed three methods which will allow you to monitor the performance of the industry groups, using *Barron's* "Industry Stock Groups" for your data.

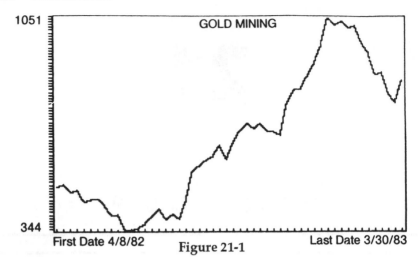

First Date 4/8/82          **Figure 21-1**          Last Date 3/30/83

The first approach plots a chart for a specified industry group showing its performance over the most recent one-year period. This allows you to easily monitor the trend of the group itself as illustrated by the example in Figure 21-1.

The second approach studies the group's performance *relative* to the New York Stock Exchange Composite Index during the same period.

These data can add greatly to your information. For example,

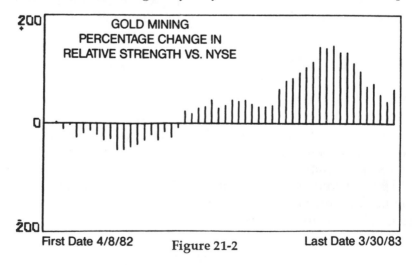

First Date 4/8/82          **Figure 21-2**          Last Date 3/30/83

while the results of approach #1 may show the index of a particular group gaining in price, the results of approach #2 might show the group to actually be lagging behind the market as a whole. On the other hand, the particular group may be seen to be in a downtrend, while examination of the relative strength chart shows that the group is still performing relatively better than the market as a whole.

Finally, when you are looking for short-sale targets, this indicator will alert you to which industries are the weakest.

Figure 21-2 is an example of the results of approach #2. Since it is in the form of an oscillator, the industry index may oscillate above or below the center line which represents the New York Stock Exchange Composite Index.

The third approach ranks each industry in terms of relative strength. A rating of 100.00 would mean that the industry performance matched exactly that of the New York Stock Exchange Composite Index during the given period. A net-change figure is also produced denoting the change from last week's reading. Whereas the charts from approach #2 give a historical perspective, the report generated from approach #3 gives a relative strength "snapshot" showing at a glance the strongest industry groups in the *present* (Figure 21.3).

**Figure 21-3**

# GROUP RELATIVE STRENGTH
## PERIOD 1 YEAR

| *Stock Group* | *Relative Strength* | *Net Change* |
|---|---|---|
| RETAIL MERCHANDISE | 183.19 | .08 |
| AIRCRAFT MANUFACTURING | 155.33 | 1.83 |
| AIR TRANSPORT | 143.65 | 8.23 |
| GOLD MINING | 139.28 | 9.68 |
| PACKING | 133.58 | 2.7 |
| AUTOMOBILES | 127.23 | -3.47 |
| OFFICE EQUIPMENT | 123.01 | 1.76 |
| GROCERY CHAINS | 119.41 | -6.15 |
| RUBBER | 119.36 | -.01 |
| TEXTILES | 117.77 | -2.35 |
| NON-FERROUS METALS | 115.63 | 2.45 |
| MOTION PICTURES | 112.93 | 5.7 |
| DOW-JONES TRANSPORTATION | 112.32 | -.08 |
| ELECTRICAL EQUIPMENT | 110.99 | -1.54 |
| LIQUOR | 107.58 | -1.85 |
| MACHINE TOOLS | 104.63 | 4.29 |
| INSTALLMENT FINANCING | 103.89 | -.05 |
| CHEMICALS | 103.82 | -1.54 |
| BLDG MATERIALS & EQUIPMENT | 102.89 | -2.38 |
| DOW-JONES COMPOSITE | 102.22 | -.55 |
| DOW-JONES INDUSTRIALS | 101.89 | -.94 |
| DRUGS | 101.14 | -.12 |
| AUTOMOBILE EQUIPMENT | 100.53 | -.04 |
| PAPER | 97.29 | -1.09 |
| FOODS AND BEVERAGES | 97.18 | -1.61 |
| TOBACCO | 96.32 | .35 |
| CLOSED-END INVESTMENTS | 93.63 | .01 |
| BANKS | 92.33 | 1.1 |
| DOW-JONES UTILITIES | 84.87 | .02 |
| MACHINERY (HEAVY) | 84.37 | .14 |
| OIL | 81.3 | -2.58 |
| RAILROAD EQUIPMENT | 80.95 | .24 |
| FARM EQUIPMENT | 79.28 | -.98 |
| STEEL AND IRON | 78.62 | -1.78 |
| INSURANCE | 75.45 | -1.07 |
| TELEVISION | 46.01 | -1.22 |

# **22**

# STOCK OPTIONS

Some of you who are reading this book may already have a good understanding of stock options and how to use puts and calls in your trading. Others, who might have computer skills, may not have been exposed elsewhere to the elements of option trading. Therefore, in fairness to those unfamiliar with the nomenclature, I will take the next few pages to introduce the reader to the basics. Again, if you are learned in this area, feel free to skip ahead to option strategies at the end of this chapter.

Stock options can be attractive as they offer investors a potentially large profit from a relatively small investment with a known and predetermined risk. The option buyer knows in advance that the most he can lose is the price he has paid for the option. There are two basic types of stock options—*puts and calls*. Let's start with calls.

**A CALL** is the right to buy 100 shares of a certain stock at a stated price within a given period of time. Common stocks on which options are traded at the Chicago Board Options Exchange (CBOE) include such well-known companies as Dow Chemical, IBM, General Motors, Eastman Kodak, etc. In all, it is possible to buy or sell (write) options on approximately 85 different common stocks on the CBOE. The buyer of the option pays to the "writer" (seller) of the option a sum of money which is kept by the writer whether the option is executed or not. This is known as the "premium."

Let's take, as an example, an "April 50 call" on ABC Company. This entitles the buyer to purchase 100 shares of ABC Company at $50 a share any time between now and April.

In the case of CBOE options, each option is normally for 100 shares of a specific, widely held, actively traded security. In the example above, ABC stock is known as the "underlying security." The $50 price at which the option buyer may elect to exercise the option is known as the "exercise price" or "striking price."

"The expiration date" is the last day on which the buyer is entitled to exercise his option to purchase or sell the stock. CBOE options expire quarterly on either a January/April/July/October cycle, or quarterly cycles beginning in February or March. All options actually expire on the Saturday following the third Friday of the expiration date.

**A PUT** gives you the right to sell short a particular stock at a fixed price. Thus, an ABC Company April 50 put entitles the buyer to sell short 100 shares of ABC Company common stocks at $50 a share any time during the life of the option.

**COST OF OPTIONS**. How much does it cost to buy an option? The premium varies with each stock and can be affected by several factors:

1.  *The time factor*. Options are termed "wasting" assets. If an option cannot be exercised at a profit by its expiration date, it becomes worthless. Thus, as the expiration date is approached, the option's time value decreases. All else being equal, the more time remaining until the expiration date, the higher the premium will be. For example, an October option for a particular stock normally commands a higher premium than an otherwise identical July option because the buyer of the October option has an additional three months for the underlying stock to move in the direction expected.

2.    *The current market price of the stock in relation to the strike price of the option*. Assume that in January an investor purchases a July 50 call of ABC Company when the price of the stock is also at $50. In such a case, the investor is only paying "for the time value" of the option. But, if by March the price of the stock has risen to $60, a new investor would have to pay a higher premium for the same call than the original investor. With the stock price at $60, the July 50 call is now called an "in-the-money" option because the market price of the stock is greater than the strike price of the call. If exercised immediately, it should yield a profit of roughly $10. Conversely, if the price of the stock were now $45 instead of $60, the July 50 call would be referred to as "out of the money" since the price of the stock is below the strike price.

3.    *Supply and demand*. Let's assume that numerous investors expect the price of the stock to rise and rush to buy calls rather than the actual stock. This automatically causes the premium to increase in value. Therefore, the price of the option is also a reflection of supply and demand for the options themselves. If the stock has been going up, there will probably be an increased demand for call options on the stock, thus making the premiums more expensive. Remember too, in such a market there is less interest in selling or writing calls by those who own the underlying stock. On the other hand, when the price of the stock is rising, put options are in less demand and are therefore comparatively less expensive.

4.    *The volatility of the underlying stock*. If a particular stock traditionally fluctuates a good deal, its option is likely to command a higher premium than the option for a stock that normally trades in a narrow price range. One common measure of a market's volatility is referred to as its "Beta." Beta is a measure of the average percentage change in the price of a stock relative to the percentage change of a market index. Thus, options on stocks with a higher beta tend to cost more. It is often for this reason that, as a general rule, premiums do not necessarily increase or decrease point for point with the price of the underlying stock. A one point change in the stock price can often result in less than a

one point change in the option premium. However, once an option reaches "parity," the premium is likely to move point for point with the stock. (For a call, parity occurs when the exercise price plus the premium equals the market price of the stock. For a put, parity occurs when the exercise price minus the premium equals the market price of the stock.)

## Option Strategies

The options market is made up of two different types of players. The first type uses the options market to reduce risk. This type—the investor or "hedger"—usually owns the underlying security; and to insure a known rate of return on his investments, writes (sells) a call against his stock. By doing so, he relinquishes the right to profit from any advance in the value of the stock during the term of the option, in return for the money he will receive from selling the call. If he feels strongly that the price of the stock may decline over the near term, he may purchase a put.

The second type—the speculator—does not usually own the underlying security and thus is termed "naked" when he buys puts or calls. He hopes to profit from a good percentage move in the value of a stock during a short period of time. Making this type of determination is much more difficult than it seems. The odds are stacked heavily against this player.

Option strategies can be extremely complex and, for the most part, are beyond the scope of this book. One good book on the subject is Max Ansbacher's *The New Options Market,* Walker & Company, 720 Fifth Avenue, New York, NY. It would also be a good idea to purchase an "Option Valuation Program," many of which are based on the "Black-Scholes Model" and are available for your personal computer. These programs attempt to evaluate a "fair price" for a given option based on the underlying stock's price and volatility.

Here are a few "general rules" to use in option trading:

1.   First, make a decision on the underlying stock before looking at its options.

2.   Be sure the stock has a high volatility factor (Beta).

3.   Select an option that offers good liquidity—in other words with a volume of at least 500 or so per day.

4.   Select an option that is fairly priced.

5.   As a rule, select an option that is not too much "out-of-the-money" nor too much "in-the-money." Usually an option that is "at-the-money" or slightly "out-of-the-money" is the best choice.

6.   Attempt to buy calls on temporary weakness in the stock; and puts, on temporary strength.

7.   Usually it is worth the extra cost of the premium to select an option with approximately six months remaining rather than choosing the nearest option.

8.   Because the time value of an option declines rapidly as it approaches its expiration date, generally it is wise to either liquidate the option or "roll forward" (sell your option and buy another three to six months forward) when there is two to four weeks remaining before expiration date. And, if you can, the ideal time to take profits is within the first half of the option's life.

# PART IV

## CYCLES

# 23

# THE MEANING OF CYCLES

Why do market cycles exist? Could it be that subatomic waves or celestial rotations somehow impact economic behavior? Or do they have a more mundane reason relating to yearly tax planning, harvest cycles, short and long-term business cycles, etc.?

Regardless of the underlying forces, our approach here is merely to accept the fact that cycles do exist in markets—for whatever reason—and to use the data empirically to improve our trading results. Cycle frequencies have been found ranging from just a few minutes to thousands of years, with countless cycles within those extremes. The key, therefore, to using cycles is to determine the *frequency* of the most critical cycles, while keeping in mind shorter and longer-term cycles as well. You would use the *critical* cycles for most of your trading decisions. The shorter-term cycles would aid you in refining your timing of entry and exit points; while the longer-term cycles help you determine the overall market trend.

Because one gains perspective from an understanding of long-term cycles, I wish to acquaint you with three very long-term cycles. A 2000-year "cycle of ages" has been identified within which exists the somewhat better-known 510-year "civilization cycle."

## 510-Year Civilization Cycle

The 510-year cycle was discovered nearly 40 years ago by Dr. Raymond H. Wheeler, Chairman of the Psychology Department at the University of Kansas. Under his direction, more than 200 researchers worked for over 20 years, studying the influences of weather on mankind. Over 3,000 years of weather were evaluated along with nearly two million pieces of weather information. Over 20,000 pieces of art were studied, as was literature throughout history. In excess of 18,000 battles were examined. No stone was left unturned.

After this exhaustive research, Dr. Wheeler concluded that the present 510-year cycle would bottom in the 1980s. He expected the "death of the world" to last until the year 2000. It was his conclusion that at the end of the 510-year cycle is when governments break down and nations collapse, and that there is a wave of international wars which are "nation-falling wars." He also expected "the initiative to pass from West to East for the next 510-year period."

## 170-Year Drought Cycle

Within the 510-year civilization cycle are three 170-year drought cycles, verified by the ring structure of 3,000-year-old redwood trees. A number of rings very close together indicates a period of drought; a series of rings further apart indicates a time of good moisture. These have tended to group into both 50-year and 170-year cycles.

At the end of a 170-year cycle, the climate turns cold and there are significant droughts. One man who has done a great deal of study on the 170-year and the 510-year cycles is R.E. McMaster, publisher of *The Reaper* (P.O. Box 39026, Phoenix, AZ 85069). He believes the 170-year cycle is also bottoming. He states: "It looks as if we are just going into one of those cold, dry cycles. The unexpected eruptions of Mt. St. Helens and El Chinchond in Mexico have added to the cooling of the climate by the debris that they have placed in the air. This and other predicted climatic changes could affect our food supply.

## Kondratieff Cycle (50-54 Years)

Kondratieff, a Russian economist, based his study primarily on statistical data including wholesale prices, interest rates, wage levels, and indexes of production for the period 1780 to 1920, using the United States, Great Britain, France and Germany as the primary models. His conclusions presented in a 1925 paper entitled "The Long Waves in Economics Life," were basically that the existence of a cycle of from 48 to 60 years in the overall economic activity of the Western world was highly probable. These preliminary conclusions have since been reinforced by the more extensive work of Joseph Schumpeter, Edward R. Dewey and others who have concluded the ideal length of the cycle to be 54 years.

Historians tell us that this "half-century" business cycle has actually been in existence thousands of years. In the Old Testament, the land was to lie fallow every seventh year; and after seven groups of these seven years—a total of 49 years—the land was to lie fallow two years in a row. More importantly, it was in this fiftieth year, the Year of the Jubilee, that all debts were to be cancelled, all indentured servants set free, and all land reverted back to the original owners—a classical "housecleaning process."

At the beginning of the 50-year biblical cycle, long-term borrowing would be common, but as the cycle began to draw to a close, money would only be available for a few years, until the forty-ninth year when only one-year loans were available. This also created a real estate cycle. If you bought some land at the very beginning of the cycle, the value was high because you could use it for 50 years; and 40 years into the cycle, prices would supposedly be much lower because you could only use it for 10 years before the title reverted to the original owner.

The pressing question today is: *Where are we now in the Kondratieff cycle?* Most economists, still hoping for many more years of uninterrupted prosperity, will deny the validity of long waves; but among those analysts that accept it—although there are differences of opinion as to the exact date of the peak—there is near unanimous agreement that it occurred in the 1970s and that we are now in the decline phase. The idealized peaks have been identified as occurring in 1814, 1864, 1920 and 1973.

Because cycles are never exact, however, it is more appropriate to look at this cycle in terms of its broad phases, which can be divided roughly into five decades:

| | | |
|---|---|---|
| First Decade | — | Recovery |
| Second Decade | — | Boom |
| Third Decade | — | Peak and Transition |
| Fourth Decade | — | Collapse |
| Fifth Decade | — | Trough and Transition |

From this perspective, we must also conclude that the 1980s represent the fourth decade in this cycle. One of the leading experts on the Kondratieff Wave is Don Hoppe, publisher of *The Donald J. Hoppe Analysis* (P.O. Box 977, Crystal Lake, IL 60014). Another newsletter publisher who is deeply committed to this field of research is Jim McKeever, *The McKeever Strategy Letter* (P.O. Box 4130, Medford, OR 97501).

# 24

# HISTORICAL STOCK-MARKET CYCLES

Just as business cycles have been shown to exist in the economy, so too have cycles been identified in the stock market. But, although their existence is generally agreed upon, the determination of when they will peak or bottom is often the subject of debate. This chapter will introduce you to some of the better research that has been undertaken in the field.

The following work on historical stock-market cycles was taken from Edward R. Dewey's classic *Cycles.* This is known as the bible for anyone interested in cycle behavior and is published by the Foundation for the Study of Cycles in Philadelphia.

**THE 9.2-YEAR CYCLE** in the stock market is well documented back to the 1830s; and it was calculated that there is only one chance out of 5,000 that these occurrences could have been coincidental. Interestingly, this same 9.2-year cycle was documented elsewhere in nature 37 different times. To be completely accurate on the average, the cycle measured exactly 9.225 years. The base year was calculated as 1832.5 and the ideal crests were timed at 3.76753 years after such cycle bottoms.

According to Dewey, the cause of the 9.2-year cycle in stock prices must be sought outside of the market itself because many other completely unrelated phenomena display cycles of this same period with crests or turning points coming at almost exactly the same time. Some such unrelated phenomena which he cited are sunspot activity, the abundance of grasshoppers and tree rings. He felt that there may be one or more environmental forces with periods at or very close to this length, and that these forces may trigger responses on the part of the various phenomena.

**THE 18.2-YEAR CYCLE** in the stock market is well documented but not quite as consistent as the 9.2-year cycle. It was calculated that there is only a 1-in-20 chance that this cycle could be the result of coincidence. Based on data through 1964, the following crests and troughs were found:

TABLE 24-1. 18.2-YEAR CYCLE - ACTUAL

| Crest | Trough |
|-------|--------|
| 1835 | 1842 |
| 1852 | 1859 |
| 1868 | 1877 |
| 1881 | 1897 |
| 1905 | 1921 |
| 1929 | 1932 |
| 1936 | 1942 |
| 1961 | 1978 |
| 1980 | 1982 |

The data of the idealized crests, the actual crests and the differences are shown below:

TABLE 24.2. 18.2-YEAR CYCLE - IDEALIZED

| Ideal Crest | Actual Crest | Difference |
|-------------|--------------|------------|
| 1833.6 | 1835.5 | +1.9 |
| 1851.8 | 1852.5 | +0.7 |
| 1870.0 | 1868.5 | -1.5 |
| 1882.2 | 1887.5 | +5.3 |
| 1906.4 | 1905.5 | -0.9 |
| 1924.6 | 1929.5 | +4.9 |
| 1942.8 | 1936.5 | -6.3 |
| 1961.0 | 1961.5 | +0.5 |
| 1979.2 | 1980.9 | +1.7 |

**THE 46-MONTH CYCLE** was discovered by Veryl L. Dunbar in 1947 and was later discussed by him in an article called "The Bull Market" which was printed in *Barron's* in June of 1952. The cycle had come true 62 out of 64 times during the past 123 years at the time the article was written, showing an accuracy of 97 percent. He stated: "In only two instances did the stock index fail to reach a higher level in the year in which the top of the cycle was reached than in the preceding low year of the cycle. Unusually remarkable, however, is the fact that the index was lower in every instance in the year in which the bottom of this cycle was reached than it was in the preceding crest year of the cycle."

Contrary to the usual conception of cycles, the apex does not fall equidistant between two lows, but instead occurs in the year immediately preceding a low. Also, the 46-month cycle seems to be "M" shaped.

The shape might possibly be accounted for by cycles 23 months in length, and perhaps 15 1/3 months in length. Regardless, Dunbar states that the cycle bottom usually occurs one year after the cycle top, suggesting that you should be long three years and short one year.

Dunbar believes that over longer periods of time, the cycles recur at intervals of 3-4-4-4-4-4 years and then repeat with six cycles recurring in a period of approximately 23 years, twelve in 46 years, etc. He also has observed similar rhythms of 23 years and 46 years in other phenomena.

**THE 41-MONTH CYCLE** is said to have been present in industrial common stock prices from their beginning in 1871. Its average length has been 40.7 months or 3.39 years. The cycle was first observed in 1912 and was secretly used by a group to successfully trade the market during World War I. Some 10 years later in 1923, a similar cycle was discovered in commercial paper rates by Professor W.L. Crum of Harvard. At the same time, Professor Joseph Kitchin, also of Harvard, discovered a 40-month cycle existing in six different economic time series.

The original 41-month stock market cycle was later rediscovered in 1935 by Chapin Hoskins of New York, who knew nothing of the earlier work.

Dewey points out that the existence of these cycles means that important highs followed by important lows tend to succeed each other with a beat and at intervals which average this length. However, it should not be misconstrued that they will succeed each other at the precise length of the cycle, in that some turning points are early and some are late.

In Figure 24-1, I have attempted to update some of this research on historical stock-market cycles. Currently, the three most dominant cycles in the stock market are the 18.2-year cycle, 9.225-year cycle and the 4.0-year cycle (discussed more thoroughly in the next chapter). Other interpretations of the timing of these cycles may be as valid as mine; only time will tell.

**JOHN HURST,** a pioneer in stock-market cycle work in the late 1960s, identified 12 dominant cycles existing in the stock market. These still exist today, though the duration may have changed slightly (see following table).

## TABLE 24.3. DOMINANT STOCK MARKET CYCLES

| Years | Months | Weeks |
|---|---|---|
| 18 | | |
| 9 | | |
| 4.5 | | |
| 3.0 | | |
| 1.5 | 18 | |
| 1.0 | 12 | |
| .75 | 9 | |
| *.50 | 6 | 26 |
| *.25 | 3 | 13 |
| | 1.5 | 6.5 |
| | .75 | 3.25 |
| | .375 | 1.625 |

*The 26 and 13-week cycles may also be viewed as combining to form what is, in effect, an 18-week nominal cycle.

Figure 24-1 S&P 500 1962-1983

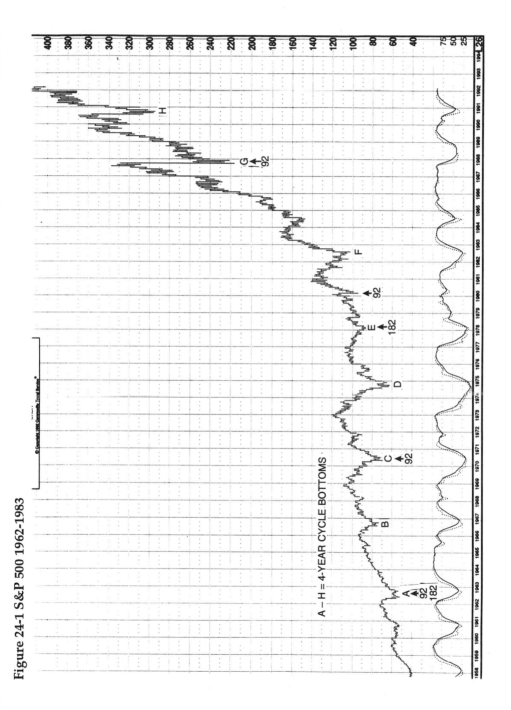

**JOHN M. COOPER,** in later works, identified the low points of the 50-month cycle (Hurst's 4.5 year cycle) and also the 18-month cycle:

## TABLE 24-4. 50-MONTH CYCLE

| Trough-to-Trough Dates | Duration |
|---|---|
| 1855-1921: | |
| Jan. 1885-June 1888 | 41 |
| June 1888-Dec. 1890 | 30 |
| Dec. 1890-Aug. 1893 | 32 |
| Aug. 1893-Aug. 1896 | 36 |
| Aug. 1896-Sept. 1900 | 49 |
| Sept. 1900-Sept. 1903 | 36 |
| Sept. 1903-Nov. 1907 | 50 |
| Nov. 1907-July 1910 | 32 |
| July 1910-Dec. 1914 | 53 |
| Dec. 1914-Dec. 1917 | 36 |
| Dec. 1917-Aug. 1921 | 44 |
| Average | 40 |

*NOTE: Between 1885 and 1921, this cycle averaged 40 months in length.*

| 1934-1974: | |
|---|---|
| July 1934-March 1938 | 44 |
| March 1938-April 1942 | 49 |
| April 1942-Oct. 1946 | 54 |
| Oct. 1946-June 1949 | 32 |
| June 1949-Sept. 1953 | 51 |
| Sept. 1953-Oct. 1957 | 49 |
| Oct. 1957-June 1962 | 56 |
| June 1962-Oct. 1966 | 51 |
| Oct. 1966-May 1970 | 44 |
| May 1970-Dec. 1974 | 55 |
| Average | 50 |

Thus, we have seen what has been done with cycles in the past. Our next step is to try to apply these same methods to the present.

# 25

# PRACTICAL USE OF CYCLES

A solid knowledge of cycles can keep you on the right side of a major trend and also give you a pretty good idea of when that may reverse.

For the "buy-and-hold" stock market investor, a familiarity with long-term cycles—especially the 4-year stock-market cycle—is usually adequate. But the more astute and active stock market traders realize that considerably more money can be made from shorter-term market fluctuations by alternately shifting from the long to the short side of the market. Such an approach, of course, demands more time and effort. What most people don't realize, however, is that the results which can be obtained via short-term trading are potentially phenomenal.

Compare this hypothetical example of *trading versus investing*. Let's say you purchase $10,000 of XYZ stock. The stock does well and by the end of the year, you have a 75 percent profit of $7,500. Your friend, meanwhile, decides to trade several different stocks, making on average one trade per month, yielding an average profit of 10 percent, resulting in a total profit of $31,380 or 313 percent per year. Why the incredible difference? The answer is *compounding*. After each trade, he was able to reinvest the entire proceeds, allowing compounding to work for him. To make it work, however, you have to (1) trade short-term so as to maximize your percent yield per period of time and (2) stay fully invested at all times.

It sounds good in theory, but does it work? The answer is yes—if your *timing and selection* are good. You must select stocks that offer a high probability of moving up or down by a good percentage in a short period of time. After you have selected a stock, you must buy it just as it begins to move. You must also have an objective of what price you expect the stock to reach and in what period of time. Then, when the stock has reached that objective, you must sell it and immediately buy another stock from among the candidates you are tracking that meet your criteria.

Short-term cycles are crucial. By identifying specific cycles for specific stocks, you can learn to predict how prices will be affected— not only in terms of the direction they will move, but also in terms of the speed and the extent of such a move.

Why do stock prices move? It is commonly believed that roughly 75 percent of stock-price movement occurs as a result of foreseeable, fundamental events influencing investor thinking. This causes the long-term trend. Unforeseen fundamental events add a random element to the market and account for approximately 2 percent of price movement. *The remaining 23 percent can be attributed to the influence of cyclic forces*—a large enough influence to allow us to construct short-term trades that take advantage of this movement.

The *duration* or *period* of a cycle is the horizontal measure from trough to trough. The *magnitude* is the vertical measure from peak to trough. Generally, cycles of longer duration exhibit greater magnitude. Cycles may also be summed together to create other cycles.

A good place to start locating and identifying cycles is in the stock market as a whole. Each stock does have its own cyclicality. But often it is very similar to the overall market. (See previous chapter for examples on how this has been done in the past.)

The next step is to take a chart of the stock market or a particular issue and, moving backwards in time, attempt to identify bottoms. You should find six or seven reasonably distinct bottoms. Measure the distance (in days or weeks) between each one and then simply calculate the average length of your cycle. A typical example might be cycles of 18, 15, 16, 14, 20 and 17 days or an average 100 / 6 = 16.67 days.

In order to project when the cycle will bottom again, we allow for 10 percent error in either direction (.10 x 16.67 - 1.67), adding this value to the average or ideal length to find the maximum days in which the cycle can be expected to bottom (16.67 + 1.67 = 18.34), and subtracting it to determine the minimum (16.67 - 1.67 = 15). Thus, we can project—with some degree of certainty—that the price will bottom between 15 and 19 days after our last identified bottom.

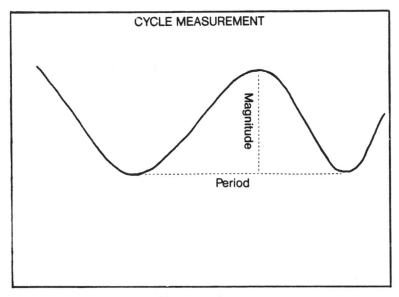

**Figure 25-1**

By adding this time dimension to our analysis techniques we have now taken a quantum leap forward in market strategy. Suppose we have picked out a stock that we wish to purchase. We believe it is in a strong bull market and have identified a 15 - 19 day cycle. Furthermore, we have determined that the last cycle bottom occurred 12 days ago. Because of our cycle analysis, we can expect the market to move lower until the cycle bottom occurs three to seven days from now. By waiting a few days we will not only be able to buy the stock at a better price but will have reasonable expectations of a swing upwards from then on.

## Enveloping

Another technique we can use to help us with cyclic analysis is called "enveloping." The object is to draw a curved channel or envelope around prices, connecting successive lows and successive highs, keeping the channel between them at a constant width. Later, you can then draw a tighter channel within the original channel or larger channel around it. These envelopes will help you to identify cycle bottoms, to visually see the general direction of the market and to set price objectives by projecting your channels several weeks ahead. Remember, prices are *generally more likely* to remain within the channel boundaries you have projected than to break out of them, but this is no guarantee they will hold in defiance of other indicators:

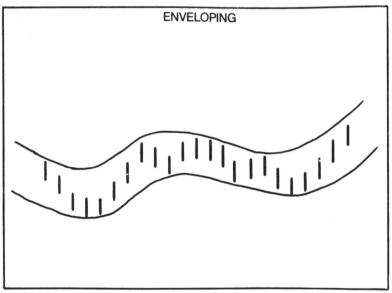

**Figure 25-2**

In earlier chapters we spent a lot of time learning about chart patterns. We learned how to identify the Double Top, Head and Shoulders, Triangle, etc. and how to use them to our advantage. We can tilt the odds in our favor by employing these patterns because they "tend" to resolve themselves in a certain manner. But sometimes the patterns abort, crumble or simply don't work.

Chartists rarely know why a pattern fails or why a pattern is successful. Most don't care to know. But the fact is that, to a large degree, chart patterns are the result of a combination of cyclic forces interacting on the price of a stock. Nearly every chart pattern, when broken down to its basic elements, contains: (1) a trend component; (2) a short-term cycle component; and (3) a longer-term cycle component. Figure 25-3 shows an example of what those components might look like separately, as well as when combined.

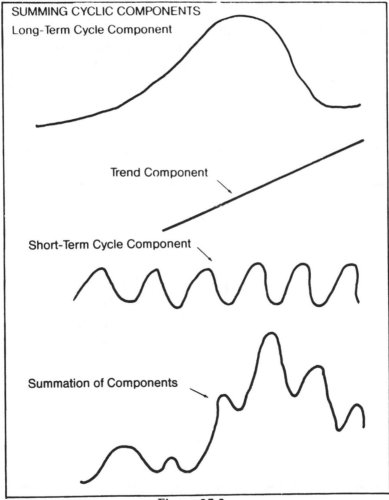

**Figure 25-3**

Voilá! We have created a Head and Shoulders pattern. We have demonstrated how it can be formed as a result of the combination of cyclic and trend components. The chartist looks for a break of the neckline to confirm that the trend has turned down. The cycle analyst realizes the trend is turning down because the longer-term cycle is topping out and will be moving down for quite some time. They are both looking at the same price pattern and are forming similar conclusions.

The chartist has learned empirically, from examination of hundreds of charts, that a break of the neckline will usually be followed by a major downward move. He must act strictly on probabilities. I feel that the cycle analyst, by understanding the reason behind price movement, has an advantage. You will see why by examining Figure 25-4. After an up move, a typical triangle has formed. The chartist, working with probabilities, knows that prices usually break out of triangles in the direction of the trend. Thus, he expects prices to go higher and soon.

But this time the chartist will be fooled. The cycle analyst will

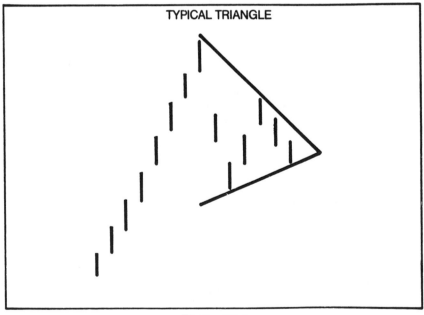

**Figure 25-4**

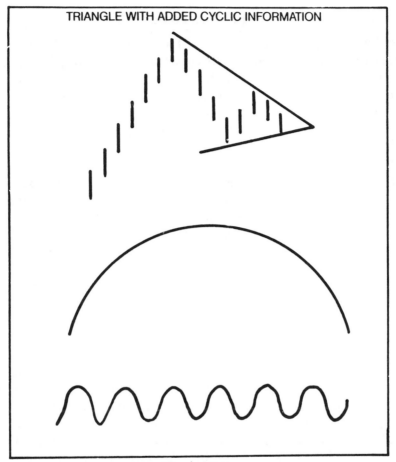

**Figure 25-5**

realize that a major cycle has just topped and is now moving down as in Figure 25-5.

Look at any graph. Can you visually "detrend" the graph—weed out the trend to examine the cycle? Or, can you "decycle" the graph in order to examine just the trend? Probably not. But fortunately your computer can do it for you.

First we will use our computer to find the trends and then to *weed out* those trends, leaving us the cycles.

## Finding Trends

Moving averages can help us view longer-term cycles (which is, in effect, the long-term trend) more clearly by eliminating the presence of shorter-term cycles. For example, a 10-week moving average will eliminate the presence of any cycles 10 weeks or less in duration. By choosing the span of the moving average, you can control which cycles you want to suppress while allowing cycles of longer length to be visible.

Going back to the cycles that we know to exist in the stock market, we can see that a 10-week moving average suppresses the 6.5-week cycle and those smaller, while allowing cycles of 13 weeks or more to come through. A 30-week moving average, commonly used in stock-market forecasting, suppresses the 26-week cycle and those smaller, while allowing the 9-month cycle and those larger to be viewed.

At this time let me alert you to an important caution about moving averages. Many analysts automatically plot the moving average in the slot for the last day of the period. For example, they plot the average for a 10-day period on the 10th day, giving you the impression that the moving average is *lagging* price changes. In cycle work, however, where timing is the main goal, it is best to *center* the moving average, plotting the 10th day between the 5th and 6th day so that stock prices and the average are time coordinated. With this in mind, it might be easier to use an odd number of days so that a stock price can be directly associated with a particular moving average. When you are purchasing a program be sure it allows you the option to plot a "centered" moving average.

A centered moving average also allows you to draw more accurate envelopes. You simply draw in your envelope boundaries at equal distances above and below the moving average line, following the same contour and attempting to find an ideal width that encompasses most tops and bottoms. The centered moving average also makes cycles of smaller duration more visible. As in Figure 25-6, they now can be seen to oscillate around the moving average in sympathy with the shortest cycle component that the average does not suppress.

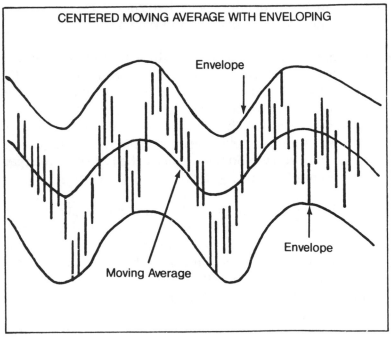

**Figure 25-6**

Here are some basic steps you can follow:

Step 1. Browse through a weekly stock or commodity chart book and select those that appear to have good cyclicality.

Step 2. Identify the major bottoms and also draw in your envelope.

Step 3. Build a data file for the issue covering the periods in your envelope.

Step 4. Using a moving average the length of your longest identified cycle, run a centered moving average on the data; and use it to further fine-tune your envelope if necessary.

Step 5.   Now try to identify one or two shorter cycles, using one of them to draw in a tighter envelope.

Step 6.   Look for *convergence*—a situation in which all three cyclic components will be turning up at nearly the same time. You should get a powerful up move during the time that those cycles are in sync. For example, if you find a 15-week cycle which has just bottomed last week, plus 8-week and 4-week cycles due to bottom in the next week or two, you would have exactly the type of convergence you need to buy a stock.

The technique works equally well in anticipation of a short sale. You identify a market in which the sum of all longer components (in other words, the trend) is down and one or two shorter cycle components are due to top in the near future. A breaking of the uptrend line can help to confirm when those cycles have topped or have started moving down—the ideal time to initiate a short sale.

Figure 25-7 illustrates prices with both a 5-week and 10-week cycle. The square represents your buy zone—the time period when

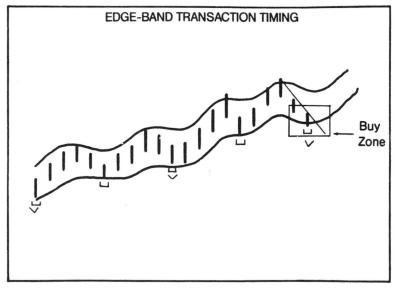

**Figure 25-7**

you expect the cycles to bottom and begin moving up. A break in the downtrend line is your signal to buy.

Your transaction is not truly complete until you do one more thing—put in your "stop"—an order which, in this instance, will limit any losses by automatically selling your stocks (or, if you're short, automatically buying it back) should prices start to go against your expectations. Not all trades can be winners and it is important that you protect your capital by cutting short any erosion you might suffer on losing trades. A safe place for your stop on this trade would be just below the recent cycle bottoms.

### Setting Time and Price Objectives

Assuming the stock does move according to expectations, the next question that arises is: Where do we take profits—when it reaches a predetermined price or after a certain amount of time has elapsed? Determining objectives in advance is a necessary part of the strategy. In order for our plan to work we must be able to evaluate risk versus reward on the amount of funds invested. We must also be able to estimate how long it will take for our objective to be reached in order to maximize our profit per *unit of time* invested.

There are several ways to measure objectives. But first you must consider the time factor. Assuming you are trading based on a 10-week cycle and that the summation of all longer cycles is up, you can expect your 10-week cycle to top approximately six to eight weeks after its last bottom. So, this is the time zone when we can expect to sell the stock.

Another way to get a rough idea of where prices might go is to extend your envelope out into the future. Your price envelope was drawn so as to include nearly all price action in the past. So, it is likely that future price action will be contained within the boundaries of your constant-width envelope projected into the future. When prices reach the top of that envelope they are likely to fall, and when they reach the bottom, are likely to rise.

Moving averages can also be used to predict the extent of a price move. You should construct a one-half span moving average. Thus, if you are trading on a 10-week cycle, you would construct and plot a 5-week "centered" moving average. When the 5-week moving average reverses its direction to up, note the price of the stock and

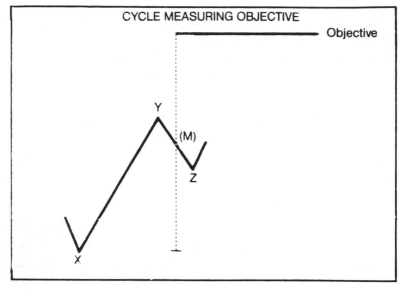

**Figure 25-8**

how much it has already moved up. You may expect prices to continue to climb until the stock has moved up this much more.

Another method is to:

1.   Use both a one-half span and full-span moving average (both centered).

2.   Project both moving averages up to current time to fill in the missing few days caused by the lag (because they are centered).

3.   At the point where they cross, note the price of the stock and how much it has moved up from its recent bottom. The stock should continue to move that much higher.

4.   Give your objective a plus or minus 10 percent tolerance for errors to set up a *target zone.*

Sometimes, although your cyclic analysis shows that prices still have room to move on the upside in terms of time, prices begin moving up strongly but then fall back somewhat forming either a flag or a triangle. This pause in upward price movement offers a good way to predict the extent of the next price move subsequent to the consolidation period. Referring to Figure 25-8 follow these steps:

1.  Measure the diagonal distance from Y to Z.

2.  Find the midpoint and mark it with an M.

3.  Measure the vertical distance from M to X.

4.  Add this same distance to M to get your price objective.

5.  If you're trading in a bear market with short sales, follow exactly the same procedure subtracting the distance to M to determine your target.

6.  Set up your target *zone* as in the previous example.


### Detrending

You have probably been wondering where your computer comes into play in cyclic analysis. We have already covered one area where your computer can save you much time and effort—moving averages. Other techniques such as envelope analysis and projecting objectives can be accomplished via manual, visual and graphic methods. But, when it comes to more sophisticated cyclic analysis such as detrending, use of the computer becomes a must.

Since the price is composed of the summation of a trend component and various cycle components, we can benefit greatly by techniques which separate the two automatically.

In the previous chapter, we found we could better see the trend by eliminating the effect of the shorter term cycles. A moving average of a specific length eliminated the effect of all cycles of that length or less, leaving only the trend and cycles of a longer length present in the data. Conversely if we want to see the cycles more clearly, we can filter out the trend. It is this process which we call "detrending."

It is actually quite simple:

*Step 1.*   Run a moving average on the data. If you select an 11-week moving average, it eliminates the cyclic information of all cycles of eleven weeks or less in length.

*Step 2.*   Subtract the moving average from the actual prices.

*Step 3.*   The result is all price movement *less* the short-term cycles—ergo the trend. Figure 25-9 illustrates the process.

**FOURIER ANALYSIS** is another way to filter out price trends. It refers to various techniques designed to extract as much information as possible from a time series of discrete numbers—including the frequency, amplitude and phase of a series of waves. This method is also called "spectral analysis."

Basically, it separates those fluctuations which have frequencies *below* a certain value from those *above* that value. When we used a moving average to filter out short cycles (high frequencies) and

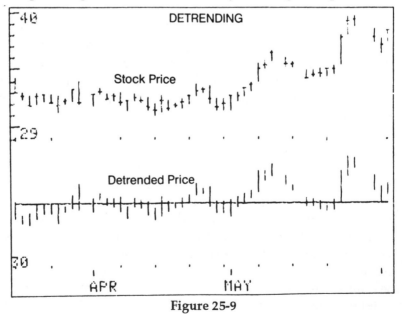

**Figure 25-9**

while allowing long cycles (low frequencies) to "pass through" we were using what is called a "low-pass filter." Likewise, when we used the detrending process, allowing only the high frequencies to show through, we were using a "high-pass filter." When a filtering process produces results that lie between two fixed bounds, it is called a "band-pass filter."

Once results have been obtained from spectral analysis, sophisticated curve fitting techniques can be applied to project those results into the future. Explanations of numerical analysis, spectral analysis, filters and curve fitting are beyond the scope of this book. However, should you have a computer, such sophisticated techniques are available to you and are worthy of later investigation.

Cycle analysis is a massive field in itself. Therefore, in order to help you avoid many hours of time and research on possibly tangential concerns, I've summarized this chapter into 15 basic steps you can follow for limiting losses and maximizing your profits. (Not every step is absolutely necessary for profitable trading. But the

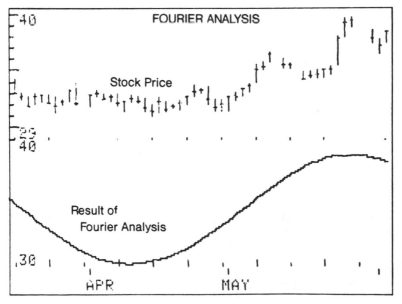

**Figure 25-10**

more homework you do which produces confirming signals, the greater your margin of certainty.)

1.   Begin by trying to identify the presence of cycles in the major averages. For this purpose, you may use the New York Stock Exchange Composite Index, Standard and Poor's 500 Index or the Dow Jones Industrial Average.

2.   Scan each of the industry groups to determine which are showing relative strength and which are showing relative weakness.

3.   Keeping in mind the direction of the averages as well as industry groups, scan the charts of individual issues and select about a half dozen that appear to have a well-defined presence of regular cycles.

4.   For each stock, project when the cycle you have identified is due to bottom next, (or in a bear market, due to reach a cyclical top.) To do this, measure the distance between each cycle bottom (or top) and average those cycle lengths. Then add the average length to the last cycle bottom allowing for a 10 percent error either way.

5.   Envelope each of the stocks to better visualize where each is likely to go.

6.   If you have one, run a detrending program to better identify your "trading" cycle and any other smaller cycles that might be present.

7.   Run a full-span moving average to suppress your cycle and allow you to clearly see the trend.

8.   Run a half-span moving average to give you another technique for projecting an objective.

9.    Monitor each of the stocks selected. Ideally, for a good "buy" signal, both the averages and the industry group should be in uptrends. Your stock should be in an uptrend as indicated by an upward rising line on the fullspan moving average. (Or for a good "sell short" signal, all three should be in downtrends.)

10.    After the trading cycle has crested and prices begin moving down, a downtrend line should be drawn. Once prices enter the time zone when the trading cycle is due to bottom, the downtrend line should be watched closely. When prices break up through the downtrend line it is time to buy the stock. Favorable volume patterns would show volume decreasing as the stock dropped in price; then increasing as it moved up through its downtrend line. (Likewise, if you're trading on the short side, the time to sell short is when prices break down through your uptrend line while falling from the cycle top.)

11.    Place a stop slightly below the recent cycle bottom (or above the recent top, if you are short).

12.    Determine an objective of what price the stock might reach and during what time period, corresponding to the crest of your trading cycle. Be sure to take into account the possible effects of any shorter or longer term cycles on the trading cycle. An objective in price can be gained from (a) envelope projection, (b) full and half-span moving average techniques and (c) the measurement technique presented. If you have time, once you've completed this work, for further confirmation refer back to other techniques for projecting objectives via chart patterns (Double Bottoms, Head and Shoulders Bottoms, Triangles, etc.) Also, take into consideration any overhead resistance that might lessen or stall the upmove.

13.    As prices move up, making a series of higher bottoms, move your sell stop up accordingly to lock in profits in the event the unexpected should occur. (And if you're short, bring your buy stop down accordingly.)

14.   Once prices have reached your objective in time and price, you can either take profits or you can wait for a break of the trend line to stop you out of the trade.

15.   As soon as you have taken profits, repeat the process on another stock which fits your selection criteria.

### Chaos Theory

The 1990s brought forth a new theory which purports to explain why markets behave as they do, or seen in another light, why markets don't behave as we think they should. This newly discovered field of mathematics gained widespread recognition after the publication of James Gleick's book, *Chaos: Making a New Science.* In it, he referred to Benoit Mandelbrot's 1963 study of cotton prices wherein he claimed that the fractal model most accurately represented the price series.

Fractal geometry is the mathematical paradigm upon which chaos theory is based. A good example of a fractal is a tree. Each branch has smaller branches which are similar to the whole tree. Another example is a coastline. It looks smooth from the air but the closer you get, the more jagged edges you can see. This self-similarity appears in market prices in the sense that, without scales to guide you, you would not be able to distinguish between weekly, daily, hourly, or even five minute bar charts.

Chaos theory goes a long way toward explaining why we can't rely on markets to form neat and rhythmic cycles for us to easily identify. The kind of spectral analysis used to find traditional cycles mathematically depends on a price series that is linear. Edgar E. Peters in his book, *Chaos and Order In the Capital Markets,* argues that markets have now been conclusively shown to be non-linear, dynamic systems. Ergo, markets, because of their chaotic nature, defy forecasts.

Lest you throw up your hands prematurely in despair, I should point out that it is not necessary to *predict* price in the future in order to make money in markets. We do know that markets trend. And we can make money by riding those trends if we employ proper money management and a technical approach that allows us to cut our losses and let our profits run.

While I don't suggest that you invite a chaos theorist and a cycle theorist to your next dinner party, the truth of market prices may lie somewhere between their respective contentions. While chaos theorists have demonstrated that weather patterns are chaotic, one could certainly argue that periodocities are readily apparent in weather. When chaos theorists are pressed, they must admit that market prices do differ somewhat from idealized mathematical fractals. And cycle theorists would certainly admit to the shortcomings of their models. And random walk theorists, who believe that future prices are totally independent of the past, are confounded by orderly trends. Just as the trend theorists are confused by meandering, directionless markets.

My own opinion is that markets are neither entirely predictable neither are they random. Probably the most confounding aspect of markets is how they mutate and change—a market once volatile settles down while another tears into a trend. It is this unpredictability that forces the trader back to the drawing board to modify his approach as markets change. Unlike other endeavors, in the world of trading we are all apprentices.

# PART V

## COMMODITY MARKETS

# 26

## Why Commodities?

It is estimated that for every 100 active stock market traders, fewer than 10 will ever venture into futures. The reason is fear. Making the switch to commodities is analogous to trading in a 10-speed for a Ferrari. With the Ferrari, you can get where you want to go more quickly. But if you're not careful, you'll kill yourself before you reach your destination. Trading commodities can seem like driving a fast car on an oily road. But the leverage afforded a commodities trader is nothing more than credit. Used responsibly, it can be a productive tool; used irresponsibly, it can be a nightmare.

I believe that if you are a good trader, you will make far more money trading commodities than stocks. Trading stocks, you are somewhat limited by the performance of the market as a whole. During a raging bull market, it is a wonderful place to be. You can sit back comfortably in your easy chair, turn on the nightly news and watch your profits accrue. During bear markets, one of three things can happen: 1) you can short stocks and make good profits, 2) you can retreat to the sidelines and collect T-bill interest, or 3) you can remain invested in stocks and get killed. Two out of those three scenerios are not desirable and it is rare to find a trader with enough luck and skill to ride the bull up and then ride the bear down. In addition to those trend years, there will be other years when the market goes sideways and you, as a trader, have wasted your time.

The more ambitious trader will look elsewhere for opportunities. Instead of allowing yourself to be captive to just one market, the stock market, why not avail yourself of as many as 25 different markets via futures. You will quickly see a world of opportunities available to you in foreign currencies, which are well known for their trends. In addition, you may wish to trade some of the following: T-bonds, Eurodollars, T-bills, Gold, Silver, Platinum, Copper, Crude Oil, Heating Oil, Unleaded Gas, Natural Gas, Soybeans, Soybean Meal, Soybean Oil, Corn, Wheat, Oats, Cotton, Lumber, Coffee, Sugar, and Cocoa. At any one time, several of these markets will be trending nicely as a result of supply/demand imbalances, weather conditions, strikes, or geopolitical uncertainties. And, as a trader, all you need to make money is a trend.

My own personal odyssey as a trader led me to commodities in the late 1970s. It was a bumpy ride for several years until I learned to respect the awesome leverage of these markets as a two-edged sword. After that, I was able to rein in risk through the application of money management principles until my equity curve eventually showed less volatiltilty than the S&P 500. And yet commodities have offered me returns that would be hard to match in the stock market.

For those of you who would like to learn more about trading commodities, I have included a Reader Services Page at the end of this book where you can request free information on my personal trading system. Now, let me detail some of the advantages that commodity trading may offer you.


## LEVERAGE

Leverage is an important component of any investment. By using only a small portion of your own capital you are able to magnify your returns. Assume that you buy a house for $100,000 and put 10% down. You sell the house for $110,000. You have made 100% on your investment since your investment was only $10,000. The $90,000 that the bank loaned you was leverage. In the 1970s and 1980s when houses were generally appreciating steadily in value, it was this leverage that magnified homeowners' returns. It was not unusual to find a young couple's net worth increase 10 fold in a matter of just a few years as that $100,000 house became a $200,000 house. Ofcourse, as many of these couples later came to realize, their net worth was only on paper. In the late 1980s the economy slowed and many people lost their jobs forcing them to sell their homes. It was a bitter pill to swallow when they realized that their net worth, primarily tied up in home equity, was not what they had expected. Thus, the leverage that had been their friend when the real estate market was advancing had become their worst enemy when prices began to decline.

Let's look at leverage in the context of other investment mediums. How about stocks? Most investors who buy stocks do so without leverage. Thus if they buy IBM at 100, the stock must double in price for them to double their money. Of course, many people buy stocks on margin. They may borrow up to 50 percent of the price of the stock. In such a case, the stock that they purchased would need to go up only 50 percent for them to double their money. I should point out, however, that they must pay interest on the money that they borrow. This money is borrowed from the brokerage firm and the interest rate is generally a couple of points higher than the T-bill rate. To compute the real profit, the interest on the loan would need to be deducted from the gross profit when the stock was sold. The same principle would apply in the previous real estate example. I will ignore the tax implications so as to keep the example simple.

Bonds may also be purchased on margin. Because the price of a bond is far more stable than the price of a stock, however, the brokerage firm will loan up to 90 percent of the price. Still, it is rare for an investor to margin his bonds. Why? Because an investor who buys bonds is generally seeking a conservative investment. Leveraging the investment to the hilt would defeat his purpose. Additionally, the interest on the borrowed portion of the invested funds would offset what he was earning on the bond, in effect turning the play into one of price appreciation only. Bond investors are generally seeking income not price appreciation.

Leverage is a very desirable quality of any investment medium. Think of it like the gas peddle on your car. It allows you to get there quicker. Would you want to drive everywhere in a car that could only go 10 miles an hour? Leverage allows you to take control of the investment like you take control of your car. Of course, mishandled, speed kills. Later, we'll see that many beginning commodity traders find trading is like driving a Ferrari. And, the failure to respect the power under the hood sometimes gets them into trouble.

## LONG OR SHORT

When you buy real estate, you can only profit if prices go up. You can only bet one way. If you think prices are going to go down, there is no way to profit if your expectations are correct. You can decide not to buy, and therefore avoid a loss, but you can't profit from prices going down.

When you buy a bond, you also hope that interest rates will go lower so that your locked in yield will become more attractive to investors and, in turn, the price of your bond will go up. If you decide to sell your bond, not only will you have collected a higher than market interest rate, but you will also reap capital gains on the sale of your bond.

If you invest in gold coins, numismatics, diamonds, or art, you can only profit if prices go higher. There is no way to profit from a bet that these investments will go lower.

In the stock market, you typically buy a mutual fund because you expect the stock market as a whole to go higher. If you buy an individual stock, it is usually because you believe that the company will prosper and the value of its shares will increase. "Wait a minute," you say. "I can sell stock short if I think the market is going down." Yes, you can. But not with the same aggressiveness that you could buy stock because you cannot margin your short sale. So, you can only participate on the short side in a limited way. Before you say it, let me acknowledge that the stock market does offer options—calls if you are bullish and puts if you are bearish. And these certainly do offer leverage. But options are a unique class of asset that is far removed from a pure play on whether the market will go up or down.

Options grant the holder the right to either purchase or sell shares at a specific price prior to the expiration of the option. Assume IBM were trading at 100 and you bought a call with a strike price of 110.

The market might very well go higher but price might only reach 109 before expiration. You would have lost your premium despite being correct that prices would go higher. So, although by using puts and calls a trader can bet on the direction of the market, he must first pay a premium for that bet and then is faced with a time limit in which his expectations must be born out. Again, the investment medium is not a pure play.

Commodities offer the only pure play where one can bet with equal vigor on whether prices will go up or down and not be limited by a time factor. Beginnners are often confused about the futures contract month which they buy or sell, thinking that their bet must end at that time. But one can easily hold onto their position indefinitely by "rolling over." This term simply means that you liquidate the futures contract month that you have when the contract nears expiration, simultaneously positioning in the next contract month. And, unlike the stock market, the same margin applies whether you go long or short. Unlike options, there is no limit as to how long you hold on to your bet nor is there a fixed strike price that must be attained before you can profit. If you believe that a market is going to go higher, and it does—no matter if it is just a teeny weeny bit and no matter how long it takes, you can profit. The same would hold true for the downside if you go short. So, besides the increased leverage that we spoke about which gives you more control, the very fact that you can control the time at which you sell—buy now and sell it 30 seconds later, at the end of the day, next week or next year—and you can control the price at which you sell—just a teeny weeny bit higher or a lot higher, gives commoditity trading the unique distinction of putting control in your hands.

Picture yourself in a Ferrari that has nothing but a gas pedal, brakes, and a gearshift with only forward and reverse. Your gas pedal is your leverage—go as fast or as slow as you like. Your brakes are used to get you out of the market whenever you want. Decide to get out, slam on the brakes and you are out of that market before your digital watch changes. Shift into forward if you are "friendly" towards the market and think it will go higher; shift into reverse if you expect prices to tumble. Sound like fun? It is, but there's one thing I forgot to mention: Fasten your seatbelt!

## MORE OPPORTUNITIES

In the stock market, when you have a bull market, 80 to 90 percent of all stocks go up. In a bear market, the same percentage go down. Consequently, you only have one bet: You think the market will go higher so you buy stocks or mutual funds. The market can either go up, down, or sideways. In two out of three of those instances you don't make money. What's worse is that you may have to wait for months or even years to find out if you were right. Time wasted if the market goes sideways. Time and money lost if it goes down. And, a reasonable return (but it won't make you rich) if prices go up. Let's say you're right or just plain lucky and you do get invested during a bull market. And, with the help of providence and/or this book you get out before the market turns south. What do you do for an encore? Stocks spend 35 percent of the time in bear markets. Even the smartest stock market investor must then be content with T-bill interest. Time wasted when serious money could be made.

Coincidently, commodities in general tend to move inversely to stocks—during periods when stocks are in bear markets, commodities are often in bull markets. Why is this relevant? For two reasons: First, an astute stock market investor could participate during bull markets, then switch to commodities during bear markets. Second, the more savvy investor will diversify his portfolio between stocks and commodities knowing that commodities will act as a hedge against his stock portfolio. Why does this phenonenon occur? The bear will often grip the stock market when interest rates are on an upswing, often the result of inflationary pressures. These inflationary pressures are frequently reflected in the price of commodities which begin to trend higher. Conversely, lower interest rates which accompany disinflation generally cause commodity prices to trend lower and stock prices to trend higher.

"But, wait," you argue. "I thought you said that I could make money in commodities whether they go up or down in price?" You can. So, you may have no reason to return to the stock market even during bull markets. But, on the whole, you are likely to make more money in commodities during bull markets than in bear markets. The reasons have to do with technical factors—one being that bull markets are more orderly, thus more easily traded, another being that when commodities sink in price to near their historic lows, price movement becomes less dynamic and more lethargic, thus offering less in the way of trading opportunities. These are markets where supplies are adequate or even burdensome and prices are reflecting that. Big money is made when supplies are tight due to weather problems, strikes, natural disasters, or geopolitical events.

Up until now, however, we have been speaking about commodities as though they were one homogeneous group, all following each other in a given direction. In fact, nothing could be further from the truth. It is far more likely to see the different market sectors following the beat of their own distinctive drummer with little regard as to how other market sectors are behaving. Further, it is not at all unusual to see markets within a particular complex going in completely opposite directions, responding to their own unique fundamentals. Commodities are a very diverse group and it is time that we examined them in more detail.

## WHAT YOU CAN TRADE

The broadest generic subdivision in commodities is between Financials and Agricultural. Financials include Metals, Interest Rates, Currencies, Stock Indices, and the Oil Complex. Agricultural include Grains, Foods, Fibers, and Meats. Let's begin with the Agricultural as they were the original, traditional commodities. The majority of the Financials are relatively new, having been introduced by the exchanges within the last 15 or 20 years. Since it seemed odd to term T-bills or Currencies commodities, the term Financial Futures was coined and soon thereafter the terms commodities and futures became interchangeable in popular jargon.

The primary grain markets are Corn, Wheat, Oats, and the Bean Complex which consists of Soybeans, Soybean Meal, and Soybean Oil. While Corn, Wheat, and Oats are primarily North American crops, a significant portion of the Soybean crop originates in the Southern Hemisphere where the growing season alternates with our own. Thus, weather and ultimately the size of the harvest on each continent affect the current price. Corn, Wheat, and Oats each have their own unique growing areas and growing seasons and thus are affected uniquely by weather. In addition, each market's price is also affected by the carry over supplies from the previous year as well as government policies.

The meat complex includes Cattle, Feeder Cattle, Hogs, and Pork Bellies. Meat prices are sensitive to demand on the consumer side as bad economic times force people to buy less meat. They are also sensitive to the price of grain—higher costs to feed the animals translate into higher meat prices. Winter storms can also cause shortages as animals freeze and transportation systems break down causing delays in getting the animals to market.

The foods are Cocoa, Coffee, Sugar, and Orange Juice. Each of these are independent markets which respond to their respective supply demand fundamentals. They are global markets in that the production comes from various areas around the world and the demand for such foods is universal. Again, worldwide weather conditions often play an important role in determining price: A shortage of rainfall in certain parts of Africa may cause Cocoa prices to trend higher; the weather in Venezuela and Brazil is important to the Coffee crop; a hurricane which cuts across Cuba could cause a sharp run up in the price of Sugar if crop damage is sustained; and, a freeze in Florida very often sends Orange Juice futures limit up for days at a time.

Fibers are the Cotton and Lumber markets. Cotton prices bear some relationship to worldwide economic conditions because, in a recessionary environment, there is less demand for clothing and textiles. Still, weather conditions, such as flooding in regions of Texas, may cause prices to rise regardless. The price of lumber is also tied to economic conditions as homebuilding is a primary fundamental which drives this market. However, there can always be surprises. One case in point occurred during the fall of 1992 when, despite a slow economy, lumber prices shot up. Can you guess why? Remember Hurricane Andrew? The destruction it wrought in South Florida and Louisiana caused a tremendous need for plywood and other wood products as the communities affected began to rebuild in the aftermath. Sudden demand in the face of stable supply causes shortages which in turn lead to higher prices.

Metals are generally grouped with the financials though it could rightly be argued that they are basic commodities, no different from the ones already discussed. The primary metals which are traded on the major exchanges are Gold, Silver, Copper, Platinum, and Palladium. Gold and Silver are, of course, precious metals and may react to inflationary fears. Copper, Platinum, and Palladium are industrial metals and are closely tied to the economy. It should be noted, however, that Platinum exhibits the same speculative appeal that Gold and Silver do, and often moves in tandem with them. Copper, closely linked to the building industry, is sensitive to the economy. Palladium, an industrial metal, is not widely traded and often avoided by traders because of the low liquidity in the market.

Interest Rate Futures are heavily traded by speculators and financial institutions alike. It is their excellent liquidity that attracts speculators to these markets. Financial institutions utilize the markets to hedge their portfolios of debt instruments. The most heavily traded markets are the Eurodollars, T-bonds, T-bills, Muni bonds, and Notes of various maturities. With global trading now available to the small speculator, the debt instruments of England, France, Germany, and Japan may also be traded.

The most popular currencies traded on U.S. exchanges are the Deutsche Mark, Swiss Franc, British Pound, Japanese Yen, Canadian Dollar, and Dollar Index. The primary factor that determines the value of a particular currency is the prevailing interest rate in that particular country. Money tends to flow toward countries offering high interest rates. However, high interest rates is only one factor that investors look at. Global investors are also concerned with the safety of a currency and whether it is likely to be devalued. Therefore, they also take into consideration the strength of the economy in the country under consideration. Countries defending weak currencies typically offer high rates of interest to attract global investment funds. But, often the high interest rate is due to a high rate of inflation in the country which in turn would continue to erode the investor's purchasing power relative to other currencies.

The stock indices have been an extremely popular financial market since they were first devised. By far the most heavily traded is the S&P 500 contract which mimics the S&P 500 Stock Index. It is used heavily by financial institutions to hedge their portfolio of stocks. Because volatile intraday swings are common, it attracts a legion of small speculators who enjoy day trading.

The oil complex consists of Crude Oil, Heating Oil, Unleaded Gas, and Natural Gas, the latter three being known as the products. There are always many factors at work which contribute to price movement in these markets: the vagaries of OPEC oil ministers, economic conditions, weather, and refinery fires to name a few. Seasonality also plays an important part in these markets. For example, the demand for heating oil is much higher in the winter while the demand for unleaded gasoline is higher in the summer, the driving season. Ever thought about what it would be like to be in the oil business? You don't need land or oil wells. You can create your own oil refinery on paper by simply buying crude oil and selling heating oil, gasoline, or both. If you think that there will be a shortage of supply of product—possibly the result of an arctic blast occurring when stores of product are low, simply buy heating oil contracts and sell crude oil to hedge your bet. You've just entered the oil business for only a few thousand dollars!

There's one last contract that allows you to bet which direction commodity prices in general will trend. It's called the CRB Index which stands for Commodity Research Bureau and represents a basket of many different commodities. It is particularly sensitive to price movement in the grains and oil complex.

## QUICKER GAINS

Due to the leverage employed, in commodities you are able to make money at a faster clip than in stocks, bonds, or other investment mediums. Needless to say, the converse is also true: you can also lose money faster. But, let's be optimistic and assume you are going to be one of those people who will make money trading commodities.

How much faster can you make money? Here are some examples: To trade one contract of the Swiss Franc requires $2,000 in margin. You make $1,250 for every point the Swiss Frank moves in your favor. It is quite common for the Swiss Franc to move five points in one month. That equates to a $6,000 return on $2,000 of invested capital, or 300 percent in one month! And that is very typical. Hardly a month goes by that some commodity won't have a sizeable move. For example, in a recent British Pound move, the currency moved 30 points in two weeks for a payoff of $18,750 on a $2,000 investment. I'll let you compute that rate of return.

But don't let these mouth watering returns cloud your judgement. It is not possible to cherry pick profitable trades while nimbly sidestepping the losers. You must be realistic and realize that, while it is not unlikely that you will catch moves like these, you must remember that you will also be incurring losses on those trades that did not go in your favor. Be that as it may, a good commodity trader has the potential to make substantial percentage gains in his account over a relatively short period of time.

How significant is that idea—quicker gains? Far more so than most would imagine. Compounding money at a high rate of interest is the key to rapid wealth accumulation. Let's look at some examples. Remember our Swiss Franc example where the payoff was 300 percent in one month? Given that it is not practical to think that you could catch those winners without incurring losing trades as well, let's be very realistic in our expectations. What if instead of 300 percent, you managed to make just 3 percent per month. How quickly could you achieve your financial goals? A $25,000 account compounded at 3 percent per month would grow to $299,410 in just 7 years, $867,774 in 10 years. Maybe you could even do a little better. At 5 percent per month, the account would grow to $1,506,056 in 7 years, $8,722,799 in 10 years. Do you know of anywhere else where it would be possible to turn 25 thousand dollars into 8 or 9 million in the next 10 years?

I hope that I've adequately answered the question posed by this chapter's title, "Why Commodities?" You can see why it is easy to get excited about trading commodities. But like wanna-be starlets stepping off the bus in Hollywood, only a small percentage of those who open commodity accounts ever achieve their dreams. Fortunately, however, unlike becoming a movie star where luck is the primary factor, becoming a successful commodity trader and achieving your financial goals has practically nothing to do with luck.

The next chapter will illustrate the potential to make huge returns quickly in commodities. So get your calculator out and have some fun playing "If only I had bought . . ." But don't stop reading there. Immediately proceed to the next chapter which explores how beginning traders go wrong and shows you how to avoid the mistakes that can derail your trading career prematurely.

# 27

# SPECTACULAR COMMODITY TRADES

Possibly not having traded commodities before, you may not be familiar with historical commodity moves and the profit potentials which they afforded. Therefore, I thought what better way to excite you about commodity trading than to give you some real life examples. After all, it is these "megamoves" which keep us commodity traders plugging along. We know that megamoves do come along, quite frequently in fact, and reminding ourself of that fact is motivational. I hope that you will find these examples inspiring as well.

Although the 1970s offered far more spectacular moves than the 1980s, I have limited my examples to only those which occurred subsequent to 1980 in order to more accurately represent today's market potentials. Because margin requirements vary over time and I cannot be accurate about a given margin at a particular point in time, you can easily assess the risk/reward on these trades by assuming a standard $500 risk on each trade. My dollar values on each move were arrived at by taking the low to high or vice-versa. It would not be reasonable to expect to capture the entire move so the exercise is hypothetical in that respect.

Besides being fun and inspirational, viewing these charts serves an educational purpose as well. This group of charts, while representative of spectacular moves, is not all inclusive. There were nearly an equal number not included that were almost as spectacular. What you may gather and remember from the exercise is that every year will produce two or three spectacular commodity moves. These moves are where the big money is made.

Just as exciting as the actual dollars per contract in movement on each of these trades is the speed at which they occurred. In most investments, we are conditioned to think in terms of annual percentage rates. But because the time required of these moves is sometimes only a matter of a few weeks, the annualized return becomes almost inconceivable. For example, the hypothetical S&P 500 move could have theoretically produced a return of 15,200 percent in 18 days which translates into 308,222 percent annualized. That's about 38,000 times better than an 8 percent T-bill rate!

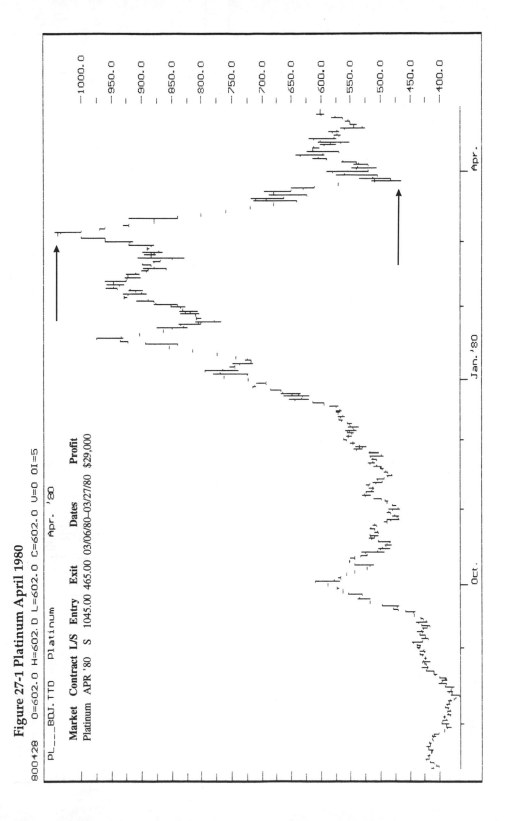

## Figure 27-1 Platinum April 1980

800428   O=602.0   H=602.0   L=602.0   C=602.0   U=0   OI=5

PL__BOJ.TTD   Platinum                Apr. '80

| Market | Contract | L/S | Entry | Exit | Dates | Profit |
|--------|----------|-----|-------|------|-------|--------|
| Platinum | APR '80 | S | 1045.00 | 465.00 | 03/06/80–03/27/80 | $29,000 |

Oct.          Jan. '80          Apr.

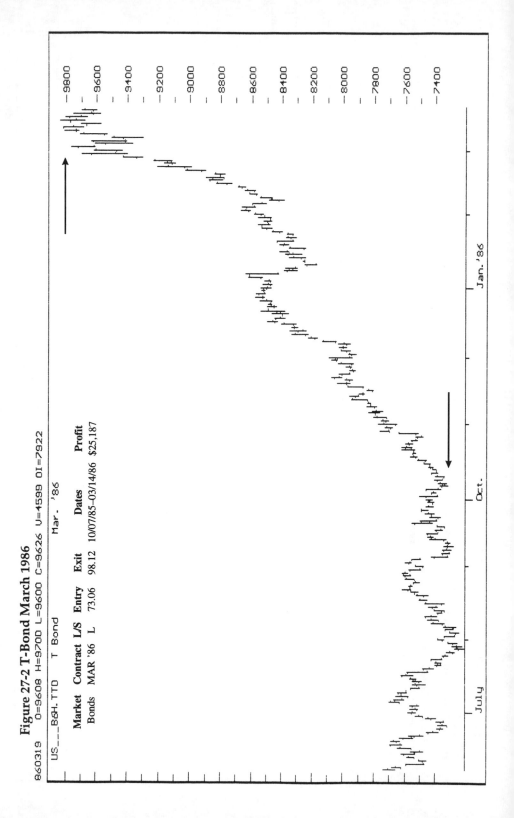

## Figure 27-2 T-Bond March 1986

## Figure 27-3 Copper March 1988

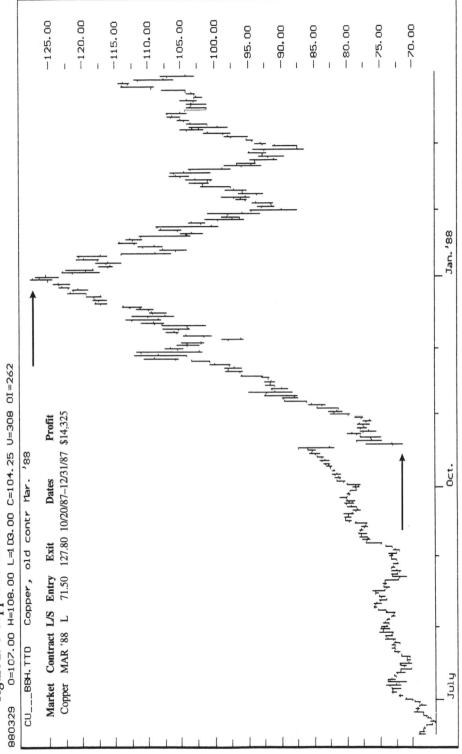

880329  O=107.00  H=108.00  L=103.00  C=104.25  U=308  OI=262

CU___BBH.TTD    Copper, old contr Mar.'88

| Market | Contract | L/S | Entry | Exit | Dates | Profit |
|--------|----------|-----|-------|------|-------|--------|
| Copper | MAR '88 | L | 71.50 | 127.80 | 10/20/87–12/31/87 | $14,325 |

Figure 27-4 S&P 500 Composite Future December 1987

871217  O=248.50  H=248.90  L=241.70  C=243.15  U=11014  OI=33648

SP___BZZ.TTD  S&P 500 Comp. Fut Dec. '87

| Market | Contract | L/S | Entry | Exit | Dates | Profit |
|--------|----------|-----|-------|------|-------|--------|
| S & P | DEC '87 | S | 333.00 | 181.00 | 10/20/87–10/20/87 | $76,000 |

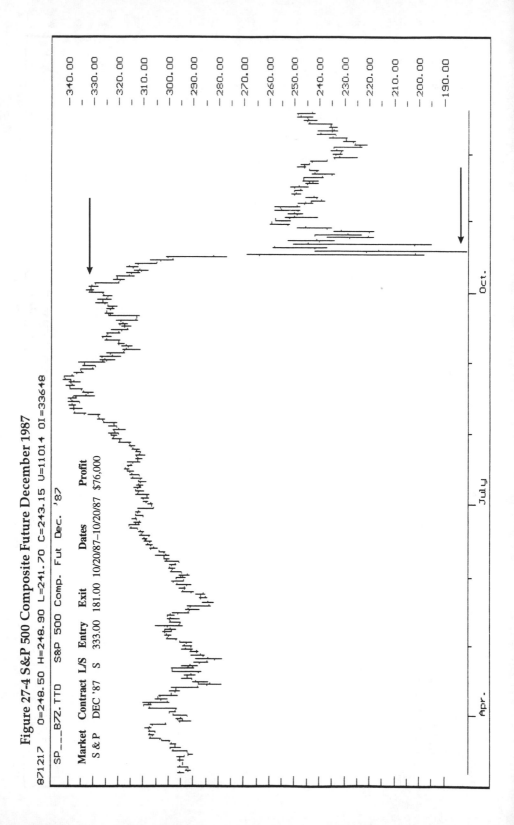

Figure 27-5 Crude Oil November 1990

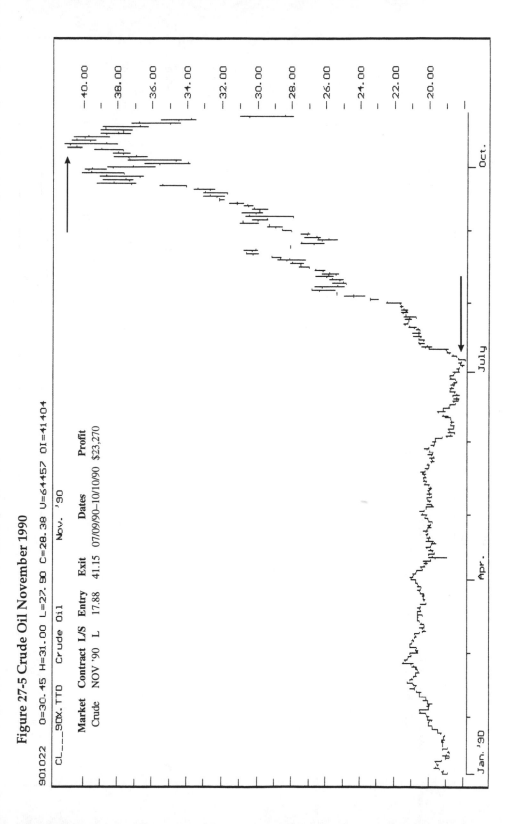

901022   O=30.45  H=31.00  L=27.50  C=28.38  V=64457  OI=41404

CL___90X.TTD    Crude Oil        Nov. '90

| Market | Contract | L/S | Entry | Exit | Dates | Profit |
|--------|----------|-----|-------|------|-------|--------|
| Crude | NOV '90 | L | 17.88 | 41.15 | 07/09/90–10/10/90 | $23,270 |

Figure 27-6 British Pound December 1992

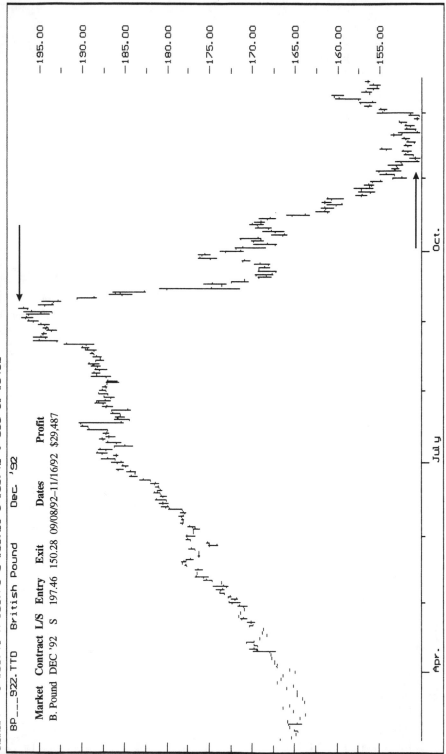

921214   O=156.40 H=156.76 L=156.20 C=156.42 U=535 OI=13462

BP___92Z.TTD   British Pound   Dec_ '92

| Market | Contract | L/S | Entry | Exit | Dates | Profit |
|--------|----------|-----|-------|------|-------|--------|
| B. Pound | DEC '92 | S | 197.46 | 150.28 | 09/08/92–11/16/92 | $29,487 |

## Figure 27-7 Corn July 1988

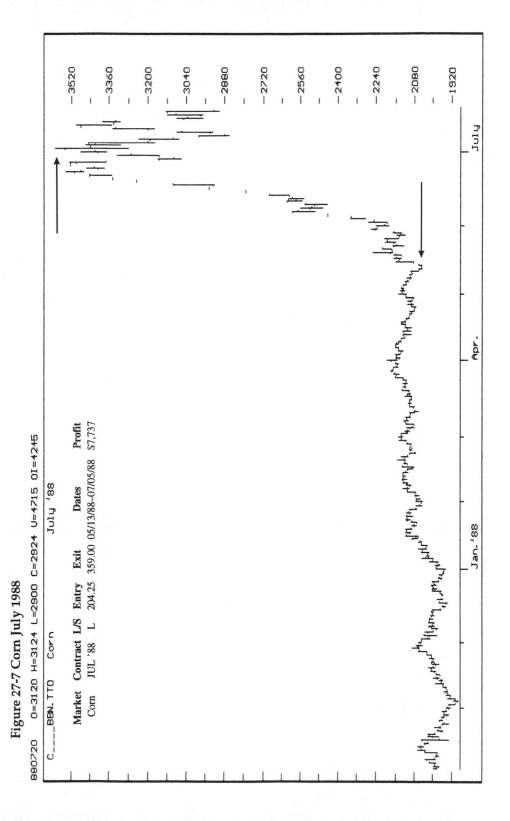

880720   O=3120 H=3124 L=2900 C=2924 U=4715 OI=4245

C____BBN.TTD   Corn        July '88

| Market | Contract | L/S | Entry | Exit | Dates | Profit |
|--------|----------|-----|-------|------|-------|--------|
| Corn | JUL '88 | L | 204.25 | 359.00 | 05/13/88–07/05/88 | $7,737 |

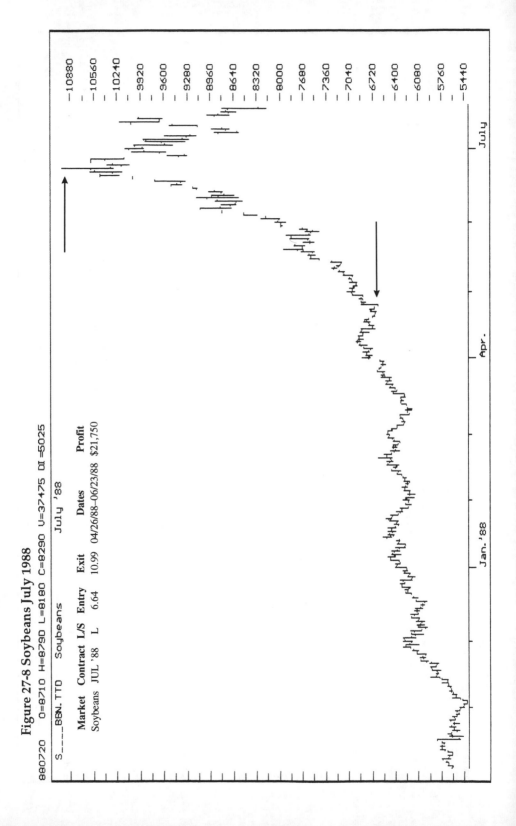

Figure 27-8 Soybeans July 1988

Figure 27-9 Wheat (Chicago) December 1991

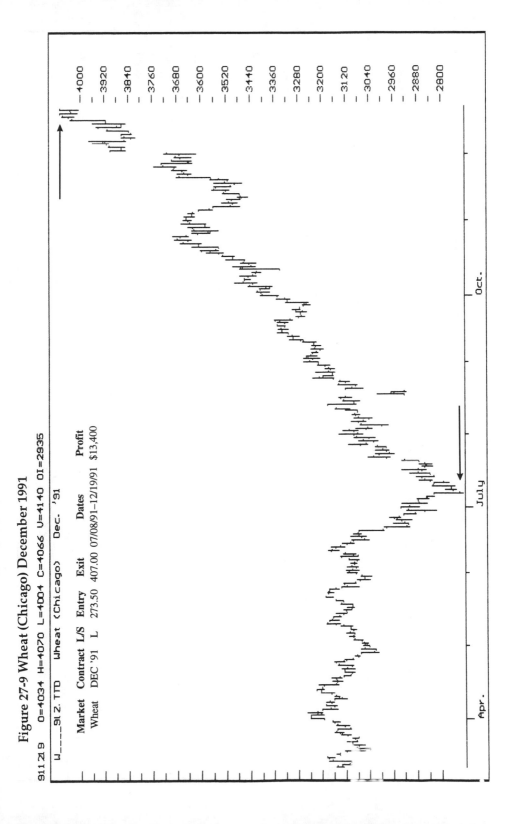

| Market | Contract | L/S | Entry | Exit | Dates | Profit |
|--------|----------|-----|-------|------|-------|--------|
| Wheat | DEC '91 | L | 273.50 | 407.00 | 07/08/91–12/19/91 | $13,400 |

Figure 27-10 Coffee "C" March 1986

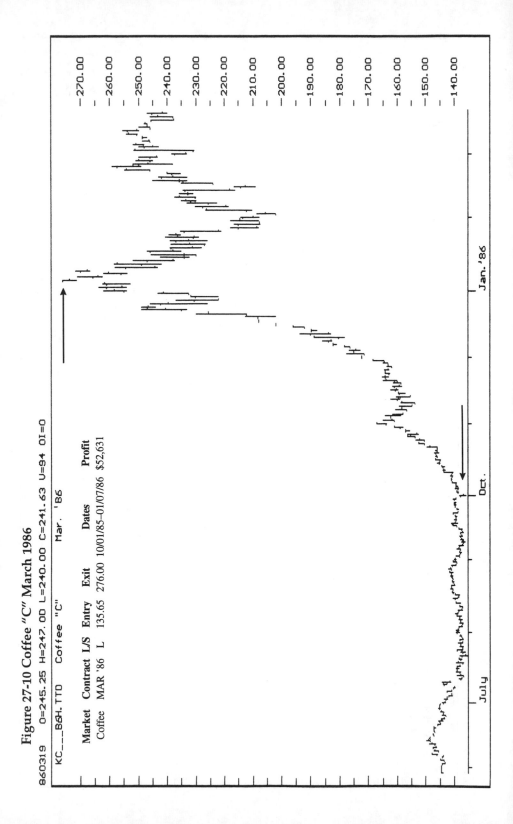

Figure 27-11 Orange Juice March 1990

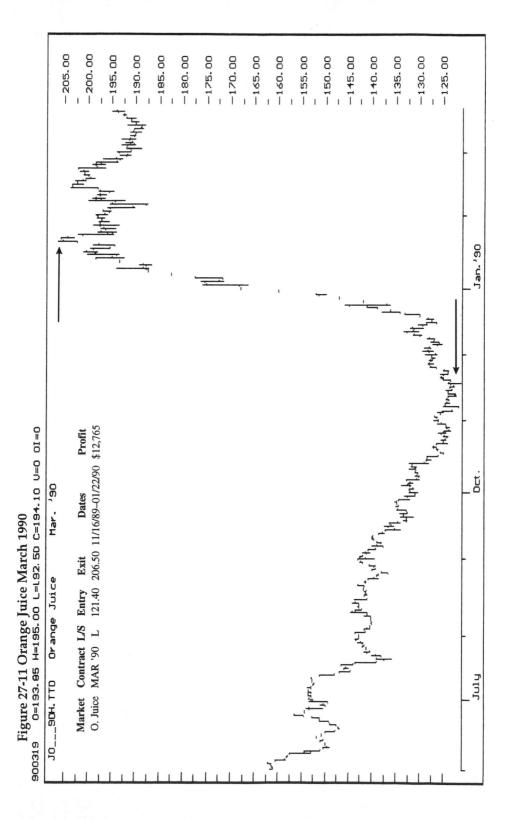

900319  O=193.85  H=195.00  L=192.50  C=194.10  U=0  OI=0

JO___904.TTD  Orange Juice  Mar. '90

| Market | Contract | L/S | Entry | Exit | Dates | Profit |
|--------|----------|-----|-------|------|-------|--------|
| O. Juice | MAR '90 | L | 121.40 | 206.50 | 11/16/89–01/22/90 | $12,765 |

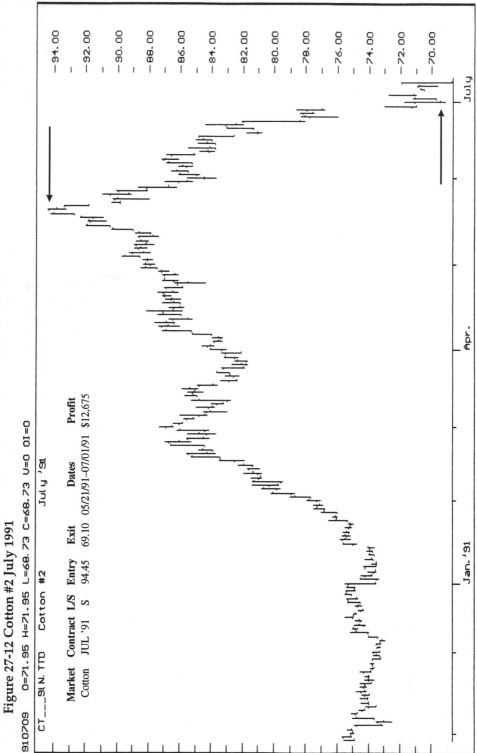

Figure 27-12 Cotton #2 July 1991

| Market | Contract | L/S | Entry | Exit | Dates | Profit |
|--------|----------|-----|-------|------|-------|--------|
| Cotton | JUL '91 | S | 94.45 | 69.10 | 05/21/91–07/01/91 | $12,675 |

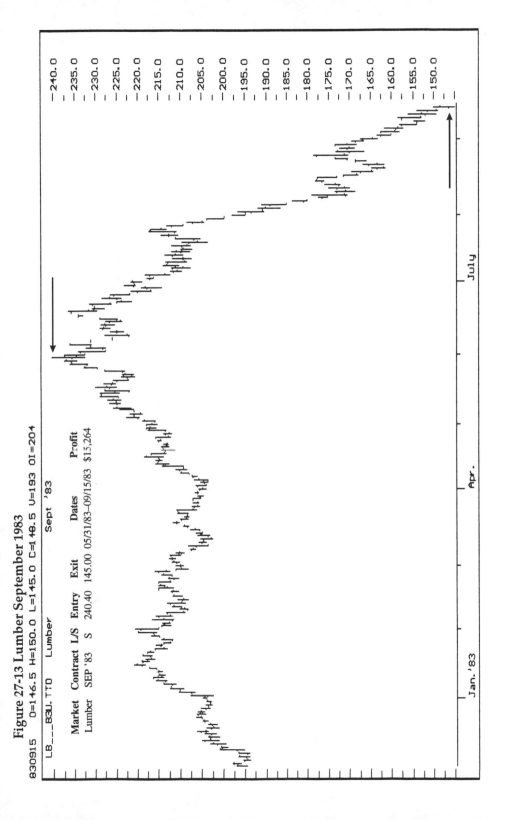

Figure 27-13 Lumber September 1983

830915   O=146.5  H=150.0  L=145.0  C=148.5  U=193  OI=204

LB__B3U.TTD    Lumber              Sept '83

| Market | Contract | L/S | Entry | Exit | Dates | Profit |
|--------|----------|-----|-------|------|-------|--------|
| Lumber | SEP '83  | S   | 240.40 | 145.00 | 05/31/83–09/15/83 | $15,264 |

# 28

## WHY PEOPLE LOSE

### THE OPTION TRAP

It is very unfortunate that, for many, their first exposure to the world of commodity trading is by way of options. I say unfortunate because buying outright options is a losing game. Thousands of people every year get stung by using this approach, never to return to futures trading. They leave the markets thinking that commodities is a "crooked" game and tell their friends and neighbors of their bad experience, who in turn are then likely to shun anything having to do with commodities because of the stories they've heard.

Despite the misguided efforts of regulatory bodies who govern the industry, a seedy subset of brokerage houses still flourish who prey off of uninformed investors, pushing their greed buttons, and milking from them money that most of these people cannot afford to lose. These brokerage operations are known as boiler rooms. The brokers who work there are usually young, unscrupulous, and may have just been layed off from the local car dealership. I have never met one who had the faintest knowledge of how to trade commodities, nor have I ever met one who cared. They are salesmen, pure and simple. They make hundreds of cold calls every day, until they reach someone on the other end of the line who is uninformed, a little bit greedy, and gullible.

These brokers are trained to read from a standardized sales script that might vary from week to week depending on what commodity is making the news at that time. For example, in my town during the Gulf War, one boiler room was making a fortune selling calls on crude oil to thousands of investors who had never traded commodities before. It even made our local news. These investors only knew, or should I say expected, that the price of oil would continue to skyrocket. It was easy for the brokers to get the public excited about the prospects for higher oil prices. What the investors did not understand was that prices had already risen substantially before they had the opportunity to buy, and, that the call options were outrageously overpriced due to extreme volatility in the market. It was like tulip mania—a classic case of a boom bust cycle. Only this time it was illustrating the herd instinct of uniformed investors, played out over a very short period of time. You may recall that the Gulf War was short-lived and, as is always the case in such cycles, the majority of investors came late to the party and were clipped as the price of oil plunged as quickly as it had risen.

Why are uninformed investors attracted to options? Primarily because options are touted as a way to make a lot of money with a small investment and because the investor's loss is limited to the price of the option. Is it true? Do options indeed offer the investor a way to make a lot of money with a small investment? Absolutely, and I'll give you a couple more ways if you are of that mindset: Take a thousand dollars, go to the track and bet on a 40-to-1 long shot to win; go to your local convenience store and buy $1,000 of state lotto tickets; or, go to Las Vegas and place the money on a Keno bet. You can make a lot of money with a small investment by doing any of these things. But, is it likely?

Commodity options lie within the same genre of investments though they rank near the bottom in expectation of profit. Here's why. With the other gambles, you would attribute your success to luck and squander your winnings on wine, women, and song. However, if you get lucky on your first option trade, the broker will convince you that it was because of his skill and he has another trade which you must do. The investor who was lucky enough to win his first time out will be drawn back to the game, convinced that he can do it again. Eventually, he will lose all his money. It would be just like going back to the race track to bet on those 40-to-1 nags every day.

The broker will try to make options sound easy. However, nothing could be further from the truth. Options are extremely complicated instruments that require sophisticated computer models to analyze and a knowledge of higher mathematics and statistics to understand. The broker selling you the options does not understand any of this. What he does understand is that he wants to sell you the long shots because far out-of-the-money options are very inexpensive. Thus, you will be able to buy more of them and he gets a commission on each one that he sells.

I hope that any time you hear the word "option" you will pull out this book, reread this section and "just say no." Now, let's see what other wrong turns the novice is likely to take that will cost him dearly.

## THE HIGH COMMISSION TRAP

Some investors who have traded stocks for years at major firms like Merrill Lynch, Pru-Bache, Shearson, Dean Witter, and others will hear about futures at a cocktail party or on the golf course, then call their stock broker the next day and get his opinion. If the stock broker is registered to handle futures, he may oblige him. If not, he may refer him to someone else in the firm who is. Either way, the investor may find he is paying a very high commission for the personalized service of a full-service broker. Because futures commissions are quite a bit lower than stocks, this might not be readily apparent.

The unwitting investor now has two strikes against him: 1) too high commissions, and 2) bad advice. It is almost impossible to be successful in the futures markets if you pay higher than a $50 commission. Most successful traders pay somewhere in the teens. Though you may not be able to achieve that, you should pay no more than the minimum discount commission that you can find where service is acceptable. Of course, when dealing with a discount broker you must be able to make your own trading decisions.

Are you ready to make your own decisions? Think of it this way. No one ever became successful in this business without making his own trading decisions. The reason is that you must make mistakes in order to learn. If you let someone else make the mistakes for you, you will eventually have to start at square one. That brings us back to the bad advice that you will likely get from the full-service broker. If you are not able to make your own decisions, you will have no choice but to ask for his advice. And, in all likelihood, your broker is not a good trader. If he were, he would not be a broker (salesman). Instead, he would either trade his own account for a living or manage money. So, if your broker wants to give you advice about trading, ask to see his own personal account statements for the last year. If he can't make money for himself, it's not too likely that he'll be able to make you money.

## THE GURU TRAP

Some traders trade through a discount brokerage and receive their advice, not from a broker, but from newsletters and hotlines. These traders are in a somewhat better position to make money than those traders in the first category. One advantage they have is that the commission rate is more reasonable. The second advantage is that the advice may be better. That may or may not be the case, however.

Because a great many novice traders receive their advice from newsletter writers, I would like to examine this category in great detail. The fact of the matter is that out of hundreds of newsletter writers in this business, only a handful have something worthwhile to say. We will address the issue of following the advice of those few later. First, let's examine the "business."

Did you ever wonder who writes commodity newsletters and why? As to who, it is usually someone who has a great interest in the markets but has never been successful at trading themselves. As to why, generally it gives this person a legitimate reason to stay involved with the markets while providing a living as well. Do you think that I'm kidding? I personally knew a very prominant "advisor" with over 10,000 subscribers to his newsletter who never traded commodities himself. Why? His wife wouldn't let him because he always lost money when he did. He did make big money, however, advising others what to buy and sell.

"But he must have made his subscribers money," you argue, "or he couldn't have stayed in business." Wrong. He never made his subscribers money. He stayed in business because he was an excellent promoter and constantly attracted new subscribers. So before you put much credence in one of the "guru" types because of their "reputation," remember that it was most likely made up by a public relations man as was his purported market calls and track record.

With regards to those few advisors who are good analysts and maybe even good traders, it is still unlikely that attempting to follow their advice will make you rich. Several problems arise. First, the average investor will not depend on one advisor but will subscribe to two or three. This approach defeats the purpose. The investor falsely assumes that by comparing the recommendations of more than one advisor, he will be able to ferret out only the best trades where all his gurus agree. Most investors who follow an advisor will quickly become discouraged after a series of bad trades and look to follow someone else who is "hot." This becomes a never ending search.

Even when an investor is loyal to one advisor, two or more problems crop up. Advisors typically like to hedge their bets so they can appear right no matter what happens. Here's a typical line used by one advisor I knew: "The market should head lower punctuated by sharp rallies." If you read that, would you know whether to buy or sell next week? Can you guess how the subsequent issue would begin? Guaranteed to begin in only one of two ways. Either "In our last issue we successfully predicted the market's current decline . . ." or "In our last issue we warned investors to be on the lookout for a sharp rally which is now occurring . . ."

Suppose the advisor is more specific and even has a hotline for you to follow. The burden then rests on your shoulders to: 1) call that hotline every day, thrice weekly, or whatever for the entire year, and 2) to take every trade advised on the hotline. Not one out of a hundred investors will do that. Instead, they will impose some filter of their own and skip some of the trades.

Once investors tire of the frustrations of following a guru, they read some books on the market, maybe attend a few seminars, and with a bit of technical knowledge under their belt, they decide to make their own decisions. Congratulations to these folks! They have taken the first step on a road that might someday lead to profits for them. But, of course, it is not that easy. Where are they next most likely to go astray?

## THE HIGH TECH TRAP

Unlike as recently as the mid-1980s, in the 90s as a result of the price plunge in hardware, computers are now very affordable and very prevalent among most professionals. The typical new trader generally owns a personal computer, performs some tasks with it, and is comfortable with it.

Because of the plethora of inexpensive charting and technical analysis packages available to the new trader, it seems appropriate for him to employ them in his approach to beat the markets.

Once into this mindset, it becomes very easy to forget the basics. He forgets that the market consists of only price, volume, and open interest—all other indicators are derivative. Often he will be duplicating his efforts—viewing five indicators where one would do. The primary problem with this multiple indicator approach is that it promotes confusion—there are always contrary indicators so he can always justify his position.

## THE DAY TRADING TRAP

Day trading is another siren's song that most often lures the trader to ruin. The attraction to day trading is that the trader feels more in control. He likes the fact that he doesn't have to risk exposure in his positions over night and can therefore "sleep better." The day trader usually requires his own quote machine—a significant expense. Typically his broker will make a lot of money but he won't.

There are several problems with day trading. Commissions are the first. Commissions eat up a large percentage of the profit. Unless you are paying rock bottom discount commissions, this factor alone is enough to cause failure. The second problem is that your competition is the floor trader and he is going to beat you six ways to Sunday. The third problem is burnout. Sometimes six hours in front of a quote screen can seem like a long day. But, the most overlooked disadvantage is that you are not able to take advantage of pyramidding techniques that allow you to make big money when fundamental trends occur.

## THE ACADEMIC TRAP

The investor who enters the futures markets with an engineering or computer background sometimes approaches the markets in a very sterile way, overlooking important aspects of trading. He is to be congratulated for his logical approach to the markets. He actually develops a system and then tests it on back data to see if it works before he puts his money on the line. This makes good sense. If the system tested well on historical data, he may then "paper trade" the system before taking the plunge.

What's wrong with this approach? On the surface, nothing. Thousands of systems are developed like this every day. The problem is that they generally do not bring their inventor the profit he had hoped for. There are many reasons why. Often the system was developed to trade one particular market. These systems generally do not last because the trading characteristics of any market undergo change over time. (I learned this the hard way. In the mid-1980s, I developed an unbeatable short-term system trading T-bonds. It worked for about six months until the bonds started trading heavily in London, causing gap openings in New York. It blew the system out of the water.)

One mistake system designers make is to not go back far enough in back testing. Another mistake is to use optimization in an attempt to improve the performance of the system. But the real problem that system designers have is not with their systems but with themselves. Usually, their weakness is that they are not experienced, "streetwise" traders, so when conditions change, they are not able to adapt.

Finally, system designers are forever in search of the holy grail. Often they abandon what might have been a profitable system in search of something better. (I confess to that one myself. In 1981-1982, I developed an elegantly simple but effective Gann-based system which I called System 101. It had been back tested for eight years and showed results ranging in the neighborhood of 50 percent to 100 percent each year. I presented the original system at a futures symposium in Chicago and the transcript was later published in a book called *Trading Strategies*. I traded the system real time for about nine months but eventually got bored with it because it was not active enough for my tastes. To my chagrin, years later I received calls from as far away as South Africa and Australia from investors who had made a great deal of money using the system.

## THE SMALL ACCOUNT TRAP

Pretend that you want to start a business. You have a good idea that you think will work. You realize that you won't make money overnight. Even the best businesses generally take a couple of years of hard work before they start turning a profit for their owners. In the meantime, you have a great deal of expense—leases, inventory, advertising, payroll, etc. Talk to the Small Business Administration and ask them what is the primary cause of failure with new businesses. They won't hesitate to tell you that it is undercapitalization. The new business owner had a good idea and he worked hard to make a success of the business, but he ran out of money before the business came to fruition.

Investors would do well to think of their futures trading as a business. But, most don't. Instead, they think that they will take a shot at it with a small amount of capital and hope that they will get lucky. What they fail to comprehend is that, by taking such an approach, they virtually assure their failure. An interesting study was done several years ago by a major futures brokerage firm. They tracked thousands of new accounts for one year in order to see what effect capitalization had on an account. While I can't remember the exact figures, I do remember that of those accounts opened with $50,000 or more, approximately 80 percent were still trading after one year. Accounts opened with $25,000 saw only about half still open. Accounts opened with $10,000 were nearly nonexistent after a year, with only about 10 percent of those accounts still open. Obviously the traders with the higher account sizes had no advantage other than capitalization. They were able to withstand drawdowns and continue trading. The smaller accounts were knocked out of the box at the first sign of adversity.

Why stack the odds against you when you begin commodity trading? Thinking that you will "try your hand" at commodities with a small account is the wrong approach. If you don't think that you are adequately capitalized at this time, spend your time learning more about trading or paper trade until you have saved up enough to open an adequately capitalized account. Although paper trading will not fully expose you to the psychological demons that will emerge once you begin trading with real money, it is a worthwhile exercise that will allow you to gain valuable experience with the trading methodology you have chosen. Hopefully, you will be able to use that time to save up money to add to your account.

Another course of action would be to find a partner. If you only have $5,000, you would dramatically increase your odds of success by finding a friend, relative, or investor who would be willing to put in another $5,000. You could also form a limited partnership and sell shares in the partnership at $1,000 each. For example, assume that you, the general partner, could put in $5,000. Then, assume that you could find four friends or family members who could each put in $5,000. You would have a commodity pool valued at $25,000—an adequately capitalized account. Most commodity pools have a cutoff of 50 percent which means that if you were to lose more than half of the initial funding, you would return the remaining monies to the investors. Given that your limited partners realize that the maximum they are likely to lose is $2,500, they are more likely to want to invest. Of course, this example presupposes that you have a workable plan to make money trading commodities. You should have a definitive trading system so that you can show your investors a hypothetical track record of how it would have performed in preceding years.

## THE HOLY GRAIL TRAP

Commodity traders lust for a Holy Grail—a trading system that never loses and will make them rich beyond their wildest dreams. Therefore, regardless of whether they are experiencing success or failure in their trading, they are constantly on the look out for something better.

"What's wrong with that?" you say. "Isn't it reasonable that the approach I have devised is not the best in the world? Certainly there are more brilliant people with more experience that have discovered a better system than what I am using. Why shouldn't I be on the look out for something better?"

A logical question and your point appears well taken. But, that kind of thinking may lead you into a trap. I have found that this trap is so engulfing that probably 95 percent of small speculators—even those with 5, 10, or more years trading experience will still find themselves mired in it. As traders, we always want to do better. Ergo, we are attracted to new techniques and trading systems which promise a better way.

The trap is this. Regardless of what trading system you use, it will go through periods when it loses money and you will experience drawdowns. It is only natural during such periods to think, "This system isn't working any more. I need to find something better." But, any trading approach demonstrates cyclicality. Chances are, soon after you abandon your current trading system, it will begin making money again. Of course, by then you are already using a new system. And, it is likely that you began using that system because of its recent superior performance. All the more reason to expect that it will soon begin losing money and, once again, you will start looking for another approach.

It is human nature for you to want to be on board a winner. But in the investment arena, where cyclicality is the natural order of things, betting on recent performance is generally the wrong thing to do. I have witnessed countless examples of this during my trading career. Advisors who write newsletters and produce hotlines see their subscription rates soar or plummet based on their most recent performance. Yet, the highly ranked advisor this year will most likely drop in the rating services next year while a lowly ranked advisor will shoot to the top.

Investors will flock to the hottest new Commodity Trading Advisor only to see his future performance fall to mediocre. But, professionals who place money with Commodity Trading Advisors have recently begun to realize it is a mistake to chase performance.

Instead, they will take advantage of the cyclical nature of performance—selecting a profitable, established advisor with a long track record and then waiting for him to experience a drawdown before placing funds. Last year, several of the more established money managers actually saw their money under management grow despite having lost more than 30 percent during a recent bad trading period!

You would do well to follow the example set by these professionals. Don't chase performance whether it is a money manager, advisor, or trading system. In your own personal trading, find an approach that you are comfortable with and that you have thoroughly tested on historical data. If you are satisfied that your system will make money over time, then decide in advance when you would be proven wrong in your assumption. If you are quite certain that, based on historical tests, your system will never lose more than $10,000 before reaching a new equity peak, then that might be a good stopping point. Monitor your real time progress against historical standards. As long as it does not exceed your initial maximum negative expectations and is performing in line with historical standards, stay with your system. Give it the benefit of the doubt. The worst thing that you can do is to abandon it prematurely. Remember, there are no holy grails. There are, however, an infinite number of approaches that will make money over time. A consistent approach is the key.

One of the more important aspects of trading is designing a portfolio. How do you decide what markets to trade? While the answer may not be the same for every trader, the next chapter will give you some guidelines to follow.

# 29

## PORTFOLIO SELECTION

When a new trader looks in the *Wall Street Journal* or opens a book of commodity charts, he quickly notices that there are more than 50 different futures markets from which to select. That is three times as many as there were just 15 years ago. And, it seems that the exchanges are adding new ones every year. At first glance, the task of selecting which markets to trade can be daunting. So, what does the new trader do?

Most start with a market with which they are somewhat familiar or one that may currently be making news. When I first started trading in the 1970s, the first market I chose to trade was Gold. I felt comfortable starting with Gold because it was a popular market at the time, I thought the fundamentals were clear cut, it was easy to find out the current price, and I knew that a one dollar move per ounce equated to $100 in my futures contract.

I traded nothing else but Gold for quite a few months. Eventually my broker encouraged me to try another market. My second market may have been Silver or T-bills. Regardless, I remember feeling that it was a giant step to try something besides Gold and worried that I was getting out of my league. The notion is humorous in hindsight due to the fact that I currently have 24 different positions on—many in global markets that didn't exist even five years ago. Some of the more exotic are the German Bund, the Nikkei Index, Short Sterling, and Natural Gas. One would think that I had intimate knowledge of the fundamentals affecting long-term German interest rates, the stock market in Japan, short-term interest rates in England, and the supply demand situation in Natural Gas. You might be shocked to know that I know none of that, that I hold no opinions in that regard, and, because I am a technically based system trader, the information that you might expect I would need to know is really of no relevance to me.

The question as to how a new trader should select which markets to trade has not yet been answered but I hope you will excuse my anecdotal digressions as we work nearer to an answer. My experience in talking to new traders is that they will often begin by trading T-bonds or the S&P 500. This, I believe, is because they feel some familiarity with these markets, having traded either stocks or bonds in the past. In addition, as with my experience with gold, the bond market and stock market are very popular markets that are always in the forefront of the news. There is never a dearth of commentors on TV who are prognosticating either a higher or lower stock market or higher or lower interest rates. Thus, it is the visibility of these markets that raises the comfort level of the new trader—there are always plenty of supportive voices who he suspects are positioned as he is. Speculators generally feel better when they know that others—especially those with credentials—are supportive of their position.

Of these two markets, the bond market is certainly the better market in which to start. There are several reasons why. First, sustained trends in long term interest rates are the norm rather than the exception. It is easy to look at historical charts of T-bond futures and find clear cut correlations with economic cycles—rising bond prices accompanying a slowing economy or a disinflationary environment and falling bond prices accompanying an improving economy or an inflationary environment. These cause and effect relationships are rather straightforward and far less convoluted than those justifying currency movements.

The size of the bond contract is also very comfortable for the beginning trader. One point on the T-bond futures contract is worth $1,000. For those with smaller accounts, the Mid America Exchange offers a contract that is one-half the size of the more common full size contract traded at the Board of Trade. Another attractive feature of the bond futures contract is that it is one of the most liquid in the world which translates into minimal slippage and a tight spread between the bid and offer. Finally, volatility is high enough to offer the trader enough action to implement a short-term or even day trading strategy. All these features contribute to make the T-bond futures one of the most popular markets with traders. Some traders—though most notably floor traders—have made fortunes without ever trading anything but T-bond futures.

With the exception of high visibility, the S&P 500 Futures lack the attractive features of the bond futures. First, the size of the contract is large—just one point on the index equates to $500. Unless day trading, the margin requirements are prohibitive to the beginner with a small account. Sustained trends are rare unless one has deep enough pockets to play with very wide stops. The S&P 500 futures contract is notorious for trapping small traders in "fakeout" moves. Although a very liquid market, prices can sometimes move so quickly ("fast markets") that excessive slippage is not uncommon. This contract should be avoided until one is very experienced and has ample capital in their account. Even then, this market requires specialized systems which are not compatible with trading most other commodity markets.

## A LOOK AT POTENTIALLY GOOD MARKETS TO TRADE

Markets change. Markets which are good trading vehicles today could be dogs by the time you are reading this book. Likewise, markets that are low in liquidity and moribund today could spring to life at some time in the future, offering excellent trading opportunities. Therefore, recommending markets that are good in 1993 may not serve you well depending on when you read this book. Instead, I will tell you what you should look for in a market. Then, I'll point out some markets that have historically proven to be good trading markets and the reasons why.

The most money can be made by participating in markets that tend to trend well. Therefore, in your search for market candidates, a logical place to begin would be by reviewing your historical charts. Select a market on which you have at least 15 years of historical data. Count how many major moves came along. How often did they occur? Were there as many in the last five years as in the prior five years? Determine from the frequency and magnitude of the moves how likely similar moves would be in the future.

What do the moves themselves look like? Are they orderly? Do they appear easily tradable? Or, do they seem choppy and chaotic? What percentage of the time are trends in force? Some markets are choppy 90 percent of the time and then exhibit spectacular but short-lived runs. Others spend longer periods of time in tradeable if less spectacular trends. These markets may be better for your trading system.

The one market sector that has excelled in terms of trendiness and profit opportunities in the 1980s and early 1990s has been the foreign currencies. These markets are liquid and fills are generally good. Another advantage is that the Mid American Exchange, mentioned earlier, offers smaller sized contracts called "Minis." The only potential disadvantage to trading currencies is that they are a 24 hour market. Prices can move considerably while you are asleep and you can find the market has "gapped" beyond your stop when the markets open the next morning in Chicago. Therefore, unless you are willing to stay up all night, you cannot be certain of your risk. Still, this one minor disadavantage should not be reason enough for you not to trade these wonderfully trending markets.

In the metals complex, Copper has always been one of my favorite markets. It responds to worldwide economic demand and can often have sudden moves as a result of labor strikes. Silver and Gold, two markets that were popular and trendy in the 1970s offered the trader little action in the 1980s. These markets typify the types of markets to avoid—those trading near historical lows that haven't exhibited strong moves in several years. The Platinum market, though still running the same course as Silver and Gold, has been somewhat more dramatic and may be worth your attention.

The oil complex, consisting of Crude Oil, Heating Oil, Unleaded Gas, and Natural Gas, is a good complex to trade. The markets are very liquid and the contract sizes are within the reach of a small trader. A plethora of fundamentals can affect these markets—everything from global demand and supply, OPEC policy, weather, natural disasters, and seasonal influences. Therefore, you don't have to wait long for something to happen which will trigger a price adjustment from current levels—i.e., a trend.

The grains are excellent markets for small traders for three reasons. First, traded primarily on domestic exchanges, the chance of large gap openings is not great. Second, the markets are extremely liquid and fills are generally excellent. Third, the grains offer some of the smallest sized contracts available. Markets such as Corn and Oats for example have extremely low margin requirements.

In the foods and fibers, each market has its own distinctive characteristics and they cannot be easily grouped. Briefly, I'll present an observation on each of these markets based on my personal experience, Among the softs, Coffee has proven to be far and away the best trending market. Cocoa is just fair. Sugar is a market I don't care for. I believe futures prices are manipulated by large commerical interests. Floor traders can also move the price an entire day's range in just a few minutes without any particular fundamental justification. Orange Juice, although thin (not particularly liquid), does offer spectacular moves (generally in the October to January time frame) and tradeable trends. In 1991, 80 percent of my profits for the year were made in one six-week move in Orange Juice. Cotton and Lumber are two more markets that are not favorites, although I do trade each on occasion. Cotton, while exhibiting long-term trends, can be quite choppy over shorter time frames making implementation of a workable strategy difficult. Lumber, a thin market, is notorious for limit moves. The meats, as was mentioned earlier, tend toward choppiness a large percentage of the time and are inconsistent in their technical behavior.

## SINGLE MARKET OR SINGLE COMPLEX VERSUS A DIVERSIFIED PORTFOLIO

Many traders feel more comfortable if they just trade one market. They feel that they can do a better job and will have less to worry about. There are pros and cons to such an approach. On the positive side, it is probably true that by specializing in just one market, you could become more attuned to that particular market. You might be able to more thoroughly investigate its price history and learn more about the fundamentals that affect that market. However, the negatives in my opinion, outweigh the positives.

First, you may be deluding yourself by thinking that you know how that particular market will behave in the future given its past. How valuable was an examination of the Silver market from 1974 to 1979 in prognosticating its behavior from 1980 to 1985? One period looked nothing like the other. Trendiness had changed, volatility had changed, and even margin requirements were different. Surely, any system or approach designed to work in the former period would not have worked on the latter. I could cite many more examples but you can satisfy your own curiosity by simply paging through some monthly charts extending back 15 to 20 years. You quickly come to the conclusion that even an intimate knowledge of your market's performance in the past will not prepare you for the future.

Another disadvantage of the one market approach is that your market may move sideways for months on end, offering no good opportunities to make money. This is time wasted—time that could have been spent trading markets that did offer profitable trading opportunities.

## SINGLE COMPLEX

Trading within a single complex rather than a single market is far less restrictive and can make sense for certain individuals. There are many cases of successful  traders who do just that. Here are some examples: Many individuals become involved in commodity trading as a result of their business. Farmers, for example, often become involved as a result of hedging their crops. Very often they will restrict their speculation only to grain markets. This makes sense because their "insider's view" of the fundamentals can give them an edge in the markets. The same would apply for those in the cattle industry. International bankers also use the futures markets to hedge financial instruments and currency exposure. Those individuals who have worked in that arena often restrict their future speculation to the financial markets, again because of their specialized knowledge. For someone whose business involves oil, that complex alone offers enough opportunity so that a trader would not have to look elsewhere.

The broadened opportunities of the complex beyond the single market is far greater than one would at first think. Most traders who restrict themselves to a complex do not only trade outright positions but spreads as well. For example, the grain trader may spread the Wheat against the Corn, the Soybean Meal against the Bean Oil, etc. The currency trader would trade the "cross rates" spreading the Swiss Franc against the Japanese Yen, the British Pound against the D-mark, etc. The oil trader would trade the "crack spread" ((2 Unleaded Gas plus 1 Heating Oil) minus 3 Crude) or spread the Unleaded Gas against the Heating Oil, etc. Also, given their intimate knowledge of the fundamentals, they will often employ "calendar spreads," buying one contract month and selling another. So, you can see that by trading a complex and employing spreads which are in effect "synthetic" contracts, the trader has literally dozens of potential trades at any one time.

## THE DIVERISIFIED PORTFOLIO

Unless you have specialized knowledge in a particular market sector, you would probably be better off to trade a diversified portfolio. You might want to include one or two markets from each market sector. Generally, if a big move were to occur in any specific market, the other markets in that sector would also come along for the ride. Therefore, it may not be necessary or even advisable to incorporate more than one or two markets from any particular sector into your portfolio. Otherwise, you may find yourself duplicating your efforts.

For example, it would make no sense to have both the D-mark and the Swiss Franc in your portfolio as their price action is too tightly correlated. Ditto with T-bills and Eurodollars. In other complexes, individual markets show less but still varying degrees of correlation. For example, when Crude Oil makes a major move, both Heating Oil and Unleaded Gas participate. However, when no strong underlying fundamental is at play in the Crude, the two "products" may trend in opposite directions for short periods as a result of seasonal considerations. The same can be said for the bean complex. A major move in Soybean prices will always carry both the Soybean Meal and Bean Oil with it. But, in other instances, the products can diverge from each other.

So far, we have assumed that your portfolio is fixed—i.e., you cannot change the composition of the portfolio. It may make more sense to work with a dynamic portfolio—one in which you can shuffle the composition depending on market events. For example, when a complex breaks into a major move, there will be one market that leads the complex and one which trails. You want to be positioned in the market that is leading. How might this occur?

Assume that it is mid-January and a record breaking arctic blast has gripped the country. Inventories of Heating Oil are low because a mild winter was predicted. Prices of Heating Oil begin to soar because demand is far greater than supply. Because it requires Crude Oil to produce Heating Oil, the price of Crude Oil will rise in sympathy. However, Unleaded Gasoline prices may lag behind and trail the complex due to the fact that driving has lessened and thus so has the demand for gasoline during this period. Look at the interest rate complex. This complex, comprised of T-bills and Euro-dollars on the short end, Notes of various maturities in the middle, and T-bonds and Municipal Bonds on the long end is in constant flux as the yield curve, reflecting a spectrum of rates between the short end and long end, flattens and steepens. All complexes exhibit similar characteristics: there is always a leader market and one which trails. A fixed portfolio that is holding a trailing market within a complex is at a disadvantage to a dynamic portfolio that adjusts rapidly to changing market conditions.

How might we construct a dynamic portfolio? Let's take the bean complex which consists of Soybeans, Soybean Meal, and Bean Oil to use in our example. Let us assume that we will use the same trading system in both cases. We will buy the market when prices exceed the highest high of the last three weeks. In the fixed portfolio, we have selected Soybeans and will ignore the other two. In the dynamic portfolio, however, we will take whichever market gets the signal first. That would make sense as that market would appear to be the leader of the complex. This example is, admittedly, elementary. But its purpose is simply to show you that you do have choices in selecting your markets. A more thorough discussion of the subject, however, would not be possible without taking into consideration the actual design of your trading system.

Once you have decided on your portfolio, you will have to learn about money management. The next chapter will teach you what you need to know about that all-important subject.

# 30

# MONEY MANAGEMENT

It is only natural that when we make an investment or trade that we tend to focus on potential profits rather than dwell on possible losses. We are often so convinced that a particular trade will be profitable that we tend to push to the back of our minds thoughts that something could go awry. But in order to be successful traders, we must face these thoughts head on. Losing trades are inevitable. It is how we manage and control those losses that eventually determines our success in the markets.

Money management is simply an assortment of techniques that help a trader minimize the risk of loss while still enabling him to participate in major market gains. Ironically, it is very possibly the most critical aspect of futures trading and the most overlooked. Whereas stock market investors can sometimes get by without it, in futures markets because of the high leverage available, it is an absolute must! Without the implementation of strict loss-control techniques, sudden catastrophic losses can quickly shrink an account to such an extreme that the possibility of ever attaining profitability becomes remote.

Once a trader fully understands this concept, he has probably learned the most important lesson in trading. Specifically: *The percent gain needed to recover a loss increases geometrically with the loss.* For example, if you lose 15 percent of your capital, you have to make a

17.6 percent gain on the balance to get even. If you lose 30 percent of your capital, it will take a 42.9 percent; and if you lose 50 percent of your capital, it will take 100 percent. The following table illustrates this point.

## RECOVERY TABLE

| Percent Loss of Initial Captial | Percent Gain On Balance Required To Recover Loss |
|:---:|:---:|
| 5 | 5.3 |
| 10 | 11.1 |
| 15 | 17.6 |
| 20 | 25.0 |
| 25 | 33.3 |
| 30 | 42.9 |
| 35 | 53.8 |
| 40 | 66.7 |
| 45 | 81.8 |
| 50 | 100.0 |
| 55 | 122.0 |
| 60 | 150.0 |
| 65 | 186.0 |
| 70 | 233.0 |
| 75 | 300.0 |
| 80 | 400.0 |
| 85 | 567.0 |
| 90 | 900.0 |

Hopefully, the table has impressed upon you the fact that preservation of capital is of utmost importance. Another example will illustrate the importance of controlling your loss of capital or "drawdowns." Examine the following table:

## DRAWDOWNS

| Beginning balance | | $10,000 |
|---|---|---|
| Trade #1 | +$2,000 | $12,000 |
| Trade #2 | +$1,000 | $13,000 |
| Trade #3 | +$4,000 | $17,000 |
| Trade #4 | -$6,000 | $11,000 |
| Trade #5 | +$3,000 | $14,000 |
| Trade #6 | -$8,000 | $ 6,000 |
| Trade #7 | +$2,000 | $ 8,000 |
| Trade #8 | +$5,000 | $13,000 |
| Trade #9 | +$2,000 | $15,000 |
| Trade #10 | +$5,000 | $20,000 |

At first glance, this example appears to show a profitable track record. The account went from $10,000 to $20,000 after 10 trades. But what would have occurred if your beginning trade was Trade #4?

| Beginning Balance | | $10,000 |
|---|---|---|
| Trade #4 | -$6,000 | $ 4,000 |
| Trade #5 | +$3,000 | $ 7,000 |
| Trade #6 | -$8,000 | WIPED OUT! |

You would never have reached the profit zone let alone the $20,000 because the "drawdown" was too great. Thus, this system is either unworkable or must be capitalized to a greater degree. For instance, had you begun your account with $20,000 rather than $10,000, you would have ended up with a $10,000 or 50 percent profit and a workable system.

At the risk of being redundant, it cannot be overemphasized that money management is without a doubt the most crucial element in commodity trading and yet it is practically overlooked by most beginning traders. Beginning traders spend 90 percent of their time and effort attempting to forecast the direction of an upcoming move through an assortment of either technical or fundamental considerations. They are so enamored with their new found toolbox of technical indicators that they truly believe that successful trading is nothing more than finding the correct mix. Then, they imagine, when all systems are "go" they will have found a sure bet.

Many traders spend years in this mindset. Despite the many failed trades signalled by their indicators, they focus on the few winning trades as proof of their worth. They believe that with a new mix or an adjustment to the parameter values that their indicators will eventually give them the ability to predict market price movements. Typically you will hear comments such as: "The four week cycle is bottoming here and the market has retraced 61.8 percent of its last move so it will likely find support right here. I'm going to buy it." "This looks like the end of the fifth wave and the seasonals are down so now is the time to sell." "We broke the trend line and I have a sell signal on my stochastics so I'm going to sell it."

Given all the technical indicators that you can apply to futures markets, you can nearly always come up with some combination that will be indicating "buy" while another combination may be indicating "sell." Novice traders often make the mistake of assuming that when they find a combination of several distinct indicators which all are flashing a similar signal to either buy or sell, that they have stumbled across a "sure thing." Then, often in a last ditch effort to gain back all their previous losses, they bet too heavily on that one trade. If that trade is a loser, they are decimated— both psychologically and financially.

I like to equate money management to Freud's concept of the superego. If you recall your beginning psychology, Freud said that the id represented our basic physical drives, the ego represented rational thought, and the superego represented our conscience. Just as the superego's job is to keep us from running amok, the role of money management keeps our trading impulses in check. And, our trading impulses are truly irrational.

We come to the trading arena holding beliefs that are counter productive to successful trading. For example, it is well known that humans wish to avoid pain. In trading, a novice trader will often attempt to avoid pain by not accepting his losses. In other words, when the market goes against his position and he is in a trade that is losing money, he will hold the position rather than closing it out. Why? It is a form of denial. If he were to close the position, he would have to admit that his trade was a failure and he lost money. It would be a blow to his ego. After all, he had invested emotional energy in that position. It was his creation, his idea, his baby. For days he watched it progress, all the time investing more emotional energy as it moved in his favor. Now, suddenly, he awakes one morning to find the market has moved sharply against him. Not only does he no longer have any open profit, the trade has now gone negative.

He is gripped by sudden fear. His "id" has taken control. He is panic stricken. But wait, his "ego" will come to the rescue.

"Get a hold of yourself," it commands.

"Can't you see I'm in pain. That was my baby. I was certain that trade was going to work. It looked like a sure thing. I needed that trade to work to make up for the five losses that I just had. I can't afford to lose on this trade too."

"Quit you're crybabying. You're only down a few hundred dollars, right?"

"Right."

"Then what are you worried about? The floor traders probably just ran some stops. The market will probably come back by the afternoon. This could still be a big trade for you. You're not going to give up that easily are you?"

"I guess you're right. I'm glad you're here to help me think rationally. I was almost ready to bail out without giving the trade time to work. Then I would have had six losses in a row and I'd have to start looking for another trade all over again."

By afternoon the market has continued to fall and our friend's small loss has grown into a big loss. The "id," unable to hold back any longer, has jumped from his chair.

"Now look what you've done! Now I've lost over a thousand dollars on that trade. I should have gotten out this morning. I'm calling my broker."

"Hold your horses," the ego placates. "You're getting too emotional. It's a good thing that I'm the brains in this outfit. Look at the momemtum oscillators on your quote screen. Oversold, right? And we've retraced almost 50 percent of the upmove. Plus, there's support on the charts just a few ticks lower. The market is due for a bounce. If you want to get out of the trade, at least wait and sell it on the rally. The market is just trying to squeeze you out. You'd be a sucker to sell out here. Are you a wimp or a man?"

The id looks at the screen again and confirms that the ego is right—it looks like the market is due for a bounce. He straightens up and sucks his breath deep into his chest. "I'm a man," he says.

"That's the spirit. And, anyway, what choice do you have? You can't afford to take a loss this big. At least if you hold on you've got a chance of getting your money back."

I hope you can see that what appears to be rational thought can get you into deep trouble when trading. Why does this happen? Tests have proven that, given a choice, people will generally opt for the possibility of a gain rather than a sure loss. As long as the position is still open, there remains the possibility that the trade could turn into a winner. You can see that human nature works against the trader in this instance. In our parable, neither the id nor the ego are capable of making the correct decision. What is needed is the "superego." Like our conscience, the superego or money management system must override the other two. It must keep the trader from destroying himself by seeing that losses do not get out of control.

"OK," you say. "I get the point. You want me to keep my losses small so that I don't get blown out of the water on one bad trade. But how do I know how much to risk or where to place my stop?"

That's what money management is all about—deciding how much to risk. Like most things in trading, however, it is a complex question with no one definitive answer. Money management is unique to every trading system because each system will generate a unique distribution of trades. Some short-term systems might be highly accurate in percentage of wins while long-term systems normally exhibit a lower winning percentage but a higher average profit to loss on each trade. An appropriate money management system for each might be different. Thorough testing of the system using different initial stops would need to be performed. Then, maximum drawdowns would have to be examined over a reasonably long trade history. Still, there are money management guidelines to which most good traders adhere.

There are two questions that you must answer. First, where should you place your stop and, second, how much should you risk on the trade. There are two ways to answer the first question. Your stop may be placed "mechanically," meaning that you have a technical reason to place it at a certain point or it may be placed solely as a function of how much you want to risk. An example of a mechanically placed stop would be placement of the stop under the previous day's low. An example of the money management stop would be placement of the stop so as to limit risk to no more than $500.

If your initial stop is mechanically based, your next step is to see how much you would lose if your mechanically based stop were hit. Assuming that it is a reasonable amount based on your account size, you would want to take the trade. If your account is small, you may decide that you are a "one lot" trader and will always trade just one contract. When your account grows larger, you will start trading two lots. This is the way most small traders approach money management. Because each market varies dramatically in value, however, your equity gains or losses over the short run are mostly the result of luck—you may have had a corn trade (small value market) do well while losing on a coffee trade (large value market). Of course, the opposite may have occurred. Over time, the wins and losses will eventually average out in the various markets so this method, while not representing the ideal, is nevertheless not problematic for the trader.

The question still unanswered is how much to risk. Years ago I remember reading commodity books that said never risk more than 10 percent of your capital on any single trade. Later, I read books that said never risk more than 5 percent. In the last few years, I've seen references in the range of 2 percent to 5 percent. It appears that those who advocated risking 10 percent are no longer with us or maybe they have grown more conservative with the passage of time. I generally recommend to my students that they risk no more than 2 percent. On a $25,000 account, this equates to $500 per trade. With the exception of the S&P 500 Index, all other commodity markets can be traded adequately on a one lot basis risking $500 or less. The average professional managing a fund or a larger sized individual account will generally risk closer to 1 percent.

For the trader who does not use a mechanically based stop, he simply decides how many points in that particular market equates to $500 and places his stop at that point. For the trader who uses a mechanically based stop, the process is a little different. He measures the distance between his mechanically based stop and his point of entry, translating that into a dollar value. He then divides that dollar value into $500 to determine how many contracts to trade. An illustration will make that clear. Assume the trader buys one contract (5,000 bushels) of corn at $5.50. His system dictates that he should place his initial stop at $4.47. As each penny in corn equates to $50, we can see that he is risking $150 if he trades one contract. He would divide $150 into $500 and conclude that he could buy not one but three contracts. The prudent trader might of course want to factor in his commission cost or even allow for "slippage" in case his stop order were not elected at that exact price. Continuing with the example, if his stop were at $4.46 he would do two contracts. What if his system determined that the stop should be placed at $4.38? His risk would be $600 not including the cost of commission or possible slippage. What would you do? The disciplined trader would pass on the trade. Remember the superego? Chances are that the market is very volatile forcing his mechanically based system to widen the stops. Unfortunately, risk has become too great for our small trader. He must ignore the pleas of his id and ego and pass on the trade.

Being able to implement that decision and many others like it is not just a matter of knowing what to do, however. The hardest part of trading is developing the discipline required to follow your plan and put it into action on a day to day basis. For that, you need cool collected thinking. The next chapter will discuss emotional problems that may arise and how to deal with them.

# 31

# DEVELOPING A TRADING SYSTEM

## BEFORE YOU START

Whether you develop your own trading system or purchase a commerically available system, you will want to be sure that your system is compatible with your lifestyle. Does the system require you to monitor the markets intraday? If so, will you need to purchase quotation equipment? Are you prepared to monitor the markets intraday? Would it interfere with your current occupation or lifestyle?

Let's assume that you have decided against a short-term trading system and have, instead, decided to go with a longer term system that will only require you to make decisions in the evening after the markets have closed. How will you get your price quotes? Have you factored in the expense? What will you do if you are away on a business trip or vacation? Is your account size large enough to take all the trades that the system signals? Will you be able to financially weather the worst drawdown that the system is likely to experience? Are you psychologically prepared to stick to the system throughout adversity or, like so many, are you simply going to "try the system out" and then abandon it if it doesn't quickly make money?

It is not worth trading a system unless you can make a commitment to it. Otherwise, you will fall into the same trap that so many others do: you will abandon the system at the worst possible time and have to start all over again, this time with less capital. So, it is critical to do your homework before hand. Make sure that you have thoroughly tested your system or approach to the best of your ability. Answer the questions that I have posed and be certain that you are both adequately capitalized and psychologically prepared to trade your system.

## WHAT YOUR SYSTEM SHOULD DO

Don't try to get too fancy. Trading is not that complex. Prices can either go up, down, or sideways. You can either be long, short, or out of the market. Instead of trying to reinvent the wheel, you should develop your system based upon general principles that have stood the test of time. Most successful traders follow the same simple rules: 1) Trade with the trend, 2) Cut your losses short, 3) Let your profits run, and 4) Use good money management. Your system should adhere to each of those principles. In other words, if it is a known fact that the best money managers in the country follow those rules, then why waste your time with an approach that runs counter to them? Instead, your efforts should be spent in quantifying those principles and testing various approaches consistent with them. Before going further, ask yourself if your system adheres to these four basic principles.

## TRADE WITH THE TREND

Trading with the trend sounds simple enough. But what is a trend? You must have a solid definition. How might you define a trend? You could use waves, support and resistance, moving averages, trendlines, etc. Possibly you might use a combination of some or all of the above. Most importantly, you must have definitive rules that tell you whether or not you are in a trend.

## CUT YOUR LOSSES SHORT

The second principle says to cut your losses short. Before you can cut your losses, however, you must first enter a trade. And, of course, you must have rules that tell you when to do it. You must also have rules that tell you what to do if the trade doesn't work. This is where you can apply the principle to cut your losses short.

## LET YOUR PROFITS RUN

Letting profits run is the principle that is applied in the design of your exit system. You must design an exit system that takes advantage of the trend. Your research should be directed to finding technical clues that will alert you to a trend change.

## USE GOOD MONEY MANAGEMENT

What is good money management? It is a set of rules that will limit your risk. Any system is subject to a great degree of variability in real time markets. Your money management system is designed to give your system a chance to work before your account self-destructs.

## THE FOUR PRINCIPLES APPLIED
## TO SYSTEM DESIGN

Using these rules, we now have an idea of what a system should look like. It will consist of four parts which are subsystems in themselves. Subsystem #1 might be called the Trend Filter. It tells us when the market is worthy of our consideration. Subsystem #2 is called the Entry System. It is usually the most complex part of the system and is composed of signals. Subsystem #3 is the Exit System and may well be the most important part of the system since it determines how much profit will be extracted from the markets. Subsystem #4 is the Money Management Overlay. Think of this system as completely separate and in control of the other systems. The decision to enter any trade must pass this final arbiter before execution is authorized. Now let's explore each of these subsystems in more depth.

## THE TREND FILTER

I feel that selecting the trend filter is the least critical part of system design. Its primary importance lies in the very fact that one can be defintive about it, therefore allowing for objective historical testing and real time implementation. Commodity prices are partially cyclical in nature and moving averages do an excellent job of capturing and defining that cyclicality. You should be thinking in terms of cycles of three lengths—short, intermediate, and long.

My system uses as trend filters one filter (moving average) which identifies the long-term trend and a second filter which identifies the intermediate trend. A short-term trend filter is not necessary as my entry signals themselves voice that element. You may have rules that require those moving averages to be trending, flat or trending, or prices to be above or below them.

If you have no idea where to start, I might suggest using a simple 28-day moving average. Only take your long signals if prices are above the 28-day moving average and vice versa for short sales. After checking the moving average for the trend, you can proceed to the more important work of finding good entries and exits. If you want to try to develop more sophisticated trend filters, I suggest that you incorporate algorithms that recognize support and resistance. For example, if we were to assume that prices rising above the 28-day moving average constitutes an uptrend, we would also want to look at the market's price structure in each occurrence. We would quickly notice tremendous variation. Thus, the particular market price structure, if defined, could complement the moving average in the filtering process.

For instance, let's take an example where prices have been in a steep downtrend for quite some time and then suddenly reverse in a V bottom, closing above the moving average. Now, compare that example to one where prices have been moving sideways in a broad trading band for months, oscillating above and below the moving average. Prices are now above the moving average but still below the top of the trading range. Are prices in an uptrend or still sideways? These examples should illustrate that simple moving averages without the aid of market price structure and support/ resistance algorithms cannot adequately delineate trend.

At this point one could also introduce other non–price-related filters into the system as well. Possible filters could include fundamentals, seasonals, sentiment, open interest, and basis relationships. I strongly caution against introducing too many filters, however. As a rule, they will cause you to miss potentially big trades. In addition, they will reduce the number of trades overall, making your historical testing less reliable. You should have extremely strong evidence to support the addition of even one extra filter.

## ENTRY SYSTEM

This is the real core of your system. It consists of all of your signals. You have to define what constitutes a signal including where your initial stop will be placed, and how and when you will get out. Your entry system and exit system work hand in hand. You cannot test your entry signals properly if you don't know how you will exit.

What are entry signals? In my case, entry signals are price patterns. But, they could as easily be technical indicators or combinations thereof. The advantage of price patterns is that it is easy to define your risk. You know exactly what price you will enter and exactly what price you will exit. When using technical indicators to time your entrys and exits, however, you cannot know in advance exactly where price will be on either of those occasions.

Subsystem #1 has declared that a trend is underway. Since you trade with the trend, your job now is to find a way to get on board without risking too much money. This is what your signals are designed to do. Early systems—some still used today—simply entered when Subsystem #1 indicated the presence of a trend. These are the too common, dumb reversal systems. They are always attempting to follow the trend up or down—even when there isn't one. During years when commodities in general trend well, these systems make money—sometimes lots of money. And so they are easily justified to the potential user. The problems arise during those years when markets are more choppy. Then, trading one of these systems is pure misery. They lose money—sometimes a lot of money.

Subsystem #1, if designed properly, should keep you out of choppy markets. Subsystem #2, your entry system, should provide quantified attempts to board that moving train we call the trend, without serious injury should the engineer suddenly shift into reverse. How many ways are you able to get on board the trend? More than one I hope.

Assume that you have a set of conditions which constitute a signal. To simplify the discussion, let's call that set of conditions a pattern. You have found a pattern which tests profitably historically. The problem is: How common is that pattern? How many times will SS#1 (trend filter) give you the green light without a corresponding signal from your entry system? What will you do if the market just keeps on going? You've missed a nice trend and a lot of potential profit. At this point, you'll probably realize that you need more patterns or different types of signals. Otherwise, you'll miss too many good trades.

How many patterns or signals do you need? The actual number is less important than the concept behind the entire entry system. In the book, *Market Wizards*, Richard Dennis was quoted as saying something to the effect of: "If you have a system, make sure it is designed so that it won't miss a major move." Disregarding risk, that would be easy to do, of course. But if you require that each of your signals limit risk and test profitably, it is much more difficult. So the game becomes: How can I be sure that I won't miss a major move and yet also be certain that my entry signal will limit my risk and test profitably? That is why you need to find several specific patterns that you can trust. This increases the likelihood that one of your patterns will occur so that you can get on board the trend.

My patterns fall into certain categories. Some patterns are used only in uptrends; other patterns are used only in downtrends. Thinking in support/resistance terms, some of my patterns are classified as breakout patterns; others are classified as break-in patterns. These types of patterns, of course, require some type of consolidation. Another classification can be thought of as retracement patterns, requiring no consolidation. Having multiple entry signals at my disposal, I am reasonably assured of getting on board a juicy trend when I see one without having to compromise myself— i.e., take unnecessary risk. That should be your goal when you are designing your entry system.

## EXIT SYSTEM

The exit system could be the most critical part of your entire system. For some sporting analogies, consider a boxer who can take a punch but can't deliver a knockout punch. Consider a football team with a great defense but a mediocre quarterback. You might think that your entry system is offensive and your exit system is defensive. But, I don't see it that way. You entry system is just one decision—you enter and you are either stopped out at your initial stop or prices begin to move in your intended direction.

Now, bring in the "A team." The exit system really has the hard job. Every single day it has to make a critical decision—stay in or get out. And every day the odds change. How much open profit is at risk versus how much potential is still left in the trade. Such questions are complex and require a great deal of work on your part. More than any other component, your exit system will determine if you have a winning system.

So, where do you begin? Remember the third great principle? Let your profits run. That would suggest that, as long as the market is trending in the direction of your trade, you leave it alone. But, if the trend starts to turn, you must be prepared to get out fast. Let's look at some standard options you might consider to alert you when to exit. There are moving averages, cycles, trendlines, chart patterns, momentum indicators, parabolics, Gann lines, Fibonacci points, retracement levels, support/resistance levels, swings, and more. You have a lot to explore when developing an exit system.

You might even consider using objectives (predefined price targets where you will exit) as well. One advantage to objectives is that your equity curve will be smoother because, when looking at open equity, if the trade is successful you will not be giving back the tail end of the trade's profits. A disadvantage is that you could potentially miss a monster trade because of an early exit.

One consideration of whether to use stops only or a combination of objectives and stops is how quickly you will pick up a new signal to get back into the trend. You should test both approaches and determine which is better for your system. An account with the ability to trade multiple contracts can generally benefit from an approach that combines both.

Your research should lead you to the conclusion that there is no one right way to exit. The best way to exit changes as market conditions change. My exit system is actually a combination of several types of exit systems—let's call them subsystems. The current market condition determines which subsystem is moved into play that day. Again with a sporting analogy, you change your defense to correspond to the offense that the opponent is presenting.

This multiple exit system approach causes my stop to do three things depending on which subsystem is dominant: Sometimes my stop will move sideways. Under a different market scenerio, my stop will trail at a fixed increment each day. And, finally, given further developments in the market, my stop will jump to a chart determined price.

There is still another subsystem within my exit system. In my opinion, it is the most important susbsystem and one that you should develop. This subsystem "takes the field" on day #2 of the trade. Its purpose is to monitor market conditions during the "incubator" stage of the trade. It is not enough that the entry system provides us with a low-risk initial stop. The job of this supplemental exit subsystem is to move the stop to breakeven as quickly as possible. As an example, you might use price, time, or a combination of both to determine when to move the stop to breakeven. If you have different types of entry signals as I do, however, you will need to modify this subsystem to correspond to the type of entry signal used for this particular trade.

## MONEY MANAGEMENT

We are finally to our fourth great principle which advised us to "Use good money management." Your money management system can be thought of as an overlay on top of your entire system. Its purpose is to limit the amount of capital that you risk on each trade so that your account will survive drawdowns. It doesn't have to be that complicated.

Most novice traders risk too much on each trade. It is not unusual to see such traders risk 5 to 10 percent of their capital on any trade. Professional traders will tend to average about 1 percent per trade. Of course, the individual trader with a small account is not able to keep his risk at that level. As mentioned earlier, I recommend that traders start with a minimum account size of $25,000 and risk no more than 2 percent per trade.

At some point, you will have to decide whether to focus on your daily equity curve or to just concern yourself with risk of original capital on a per trade basis. For all but professional traders, the latter will suffice. I look at each trade as a discreet event. My primary concern focuses on the risk during the first few days of a trade. Once my trade is profitable, my money management system steps back and my exit system takes over.

## ADVANTAGES OF MULTIPLE CONTRACTS

Let's assume that you start your account with $25,000. And you have decided that, given your normal risk parameters, you will generally be able to trade one contract of a given commodity. Because your system is a good one, your account grows quickly. When do you start to trade two contracts? If your answer is when your account reaches $50,000, it leads us to the following anomaly. If your account is at $45,000 and you trade one contract, you are now substantially undertrading relative to when you first began.

Your money management system and indeed even your entire trading system needs to adjust once you reach the point where multiple contracts are called for. Problems, such as the one just illustrated, do arise. But the opportunities which present themselves outweigh the inconveniences. At this point, you no longer need to deal in the black and white world of the one lot trader who must be either 100 percent committed or out completely.

Shades of grey are now possible and a whole new world of discretion opens up. You may wish to be 100 percent committed when you encounter an exceptionally good signal. Other signals may dictate a less aggressive posture. It is your exit system, however, where modification will yield the best results. Instead of exiting your entire position on one signal, you may now take your profit in stages. For example, a loss of market momentum may cause you to reduce your position by 20 percent. A break of minor support may cause a 40 percent reduction. In other words, you are gradually decreasing market exposure as evidence mounts that the trend is about to change.

Once you are in a multiple contract environment, it would probably be wise to consider incorporating objectives into your exit system. You may wish to exit 20 percent to 50 percent of your position at predefined objectives. This allows you to exit a portion of your position (long) on strength, thus smoothing your equity curve. You can see that multiple contracts open up a lot of new possibilities to system designers. I believe that any system can be improved by employing a multiple contract approach.

You may now feel as I do that no system is ever completely finished. It can always be improved. There is always more work to do. You will learn something every time you design a trading system—even if the system does not test profitable. It is the accumulation of knowledge from the process of designing and testing that will eventually allow you to create your own masterpiece.

Odd as it might seem, having a good system or trading plan is only half the battle. Maintaining the discipline to follow your trading plan consistently is equally important. The final chapter will explore how your emotions work to destabilize your trading efforts, and hopefully provide you with the insight needed to eliminate emotionally based trading decisions.

# 32

# PSYCHOLOGICAL CONSIDERATIONS

Unless you have traded commodities before, you will likely under-estimate the importance of the psychological aspects of the game. After all, it certainly seems easy enough: You examine the charts, create a system, buy when the system says to buy and sell when it says to sell. What could be hard about that? I don't know that I have a good answer to that question but I know that it is. In fact, if you ask any professional trader what the most difficult part of trading is, he will tell you that it is the psychological aspects—or, put another way, not allowing your emotions to interfere with your trading. Let's examine some typical ways in which your emotions could affect your trading.

Let's assume first that you do have a set of rules that guide you in your decision making and that you are not simply trading by the seat of your pants. Your rules tell you when to get into a market, how much to risk, and when to get out. Here we go: Case #1. You went short Crude Oil yesterday because it appears to be in a downtrend and your system gave a signal. You place a stop 50 cents from your entry, risking $500. So far, the market is trading about where you went short. On the evening news, you hear that one of the OPEC ministers is planning to ask for a cut in production by fellow OPEC members at next week's meeting. The next morning, the price of Crude is 35 cents higher and you are holding a $350 loss. You assume that the market will continue higher so you cover your position and accept the $350 loss. An hour later, the market is 45 cents higher than where you first entered and you pat yourself on the back for cutting your losses. Then, a news flash indicates that the OPEC rumor was completely unfounded. Prices plummet and in another two weeks, they are $3.00 lower. You should have made $3,000 but instead you lost $350. Case #2. You have just suffered eight losing trades in a row. Your total losses exceeded $4,000. Fortunately, you're long the T-bonds and they've been going straight up for the last two weeks. You bought them at 90.00 and they're now trading at 94.04. You have a little over $4,000 in open profit. The T-bonds are overdue for a correction. "Why take a chance of giving back all that open profit?" you reason. You liquidate your position. The bonds continue higher over the next several days. Soon they are trading at 96.16 and the news is very bullish. You kick yourself for getting out too soon and are determined to not let any more of the move get away from you. You buy despite not having any good place for a stop. The market starts to drop. You can't believe it. You realize that you haven't put in a stop. "It's only a correction," you tell yourself. "The market deserves a little correction. If I get out I might not be able to get back in." The correction has turned into a rout. In only a couple of days you have lost more than $2,000 dollars. You're shell shocked. "How could this be happening to me?" you cry. "Please, God, just let me get back to breakeven and I promise never to do something stupid like that again." Your plea falls upon deaf ears and you eventually liquidate with a $2,500 loss, cursing the irrationality of the market. Had you followed your system to the letter, you would have finished the month with a $1,200 gain. Instead, you lost $2,500.

These two cases are very typical but in no way inclusive of the myriad ways in which the markets can cause you to deviate from your prearranged trading plan. Despite having a trading plan, the new trader succumbs quite easily to outside influences, assuming that some authority knows more than he does about the imminent direction of prices. You must steel yourself against these external influences and follow your rules to the letter. Otherwise, they will be of no use to you. What good is a trading plan if you don't follow it?

Over ten years ago, a well-known system developer taught a

trading system to a large number of seminar attendees who paid thousands of dollars to learn it. One year later, third party monitoring had shown the system had done extremely well since being taught at the seminar. Yet, incredibly, a survey of those attendees showed that less than 10 percent were still using the system only one year later. I have talked to hundreds of system traders over the past few years and I am not at all surprised by those statistics. I am constantly amazed by conversations with traders who, despite owning several high-priced trading systems, have yet to find market success. The reason has little to do with the systems they own, but has a lot to do with their own discipline. I suspect that as soon as the new system they are using experiences a drawdown, they buy another system. Consequently, they are giving up too soon, losing money, and then starting again with what they hope will be a better system. This cycle repeats itself until the trader either becomes discouraged and quits trading or recognizes his problem.

We can conclude by saying that even a good trading system is not enough. The discipline to follow the system is equally important. There will be times when you think you can do better than your system. While that may or may not be true on a particular trade or even a series of trades, it is not likely to be true over the long run. The whole point of having a system is to enable you to approach the markets in a consistent manner. If you find yourself overriding your system, you are defeating your purpose—your approach will no longer be consistent.

The most difficult decision I had to make while writing this section on commodities was whether to address only the basics or more worthwhile, advanced themes. I hope that I've been able to do a bit of both. Had I spent too much time on topics such as "What is a Futures Contract?" and "How to Place an Order," those who already trade commodities would have felt short changed. Therefore, if you have not traded commodities before, I wish to caution you that the material presented here was not intended to represent a complete introduction to commodity trading. I would strongly urge you to seek further education before committing your capital. Most major brokerage houses can provide you with free literature. Many valuable free publications are available from the Chicago Board of Trade, Marketing Department, LaSalle at Jackson, Chicago,

Illinois 60604. Don't overlook your local library as a source for books on commodity trading. Finally, I recommend a subscription to *Futures Magazine*, 219 Parkade, Cedar Falls, Iowa 50613.

If you are among those readers who have not traded commodities before, I hope that I was able to excite you about the subject and interest you in learning more. The chapters "Why Commodities?" and "Spectacular Commodity Moves" were written just for you. Those of you who are beginners will most likely identify with and appreciate the chapter titled "Why People Lose." The remaining chapters, "Portfolio Selection," "Money Management," "Developing a Trading system," and "Psychological Considerations" will be applicable regardless of your experience level.

My choice of topics was also eclectic. Much of the material you will not find elsewhere in commodity literature. And, those ideas that are shared elsewhere have been filtered by my own experience and are crystalized for your consumption. Hopefully, if you are just now becoming involved in commodity trading, you will be able to pull your copy of *Timing the Market* off your shelf next year or the year after, reread this section on commodities with deeper insight and gain still more value from the book. That is my hope. Good Luck!

# INDEX

## Reader Services Card

I would like to learn more about Curtis Arnold's approach to commodities and the trading system that he uses. Please send me information on:

☐ PPS Training - Learn Pattern Probability Strategy, Curtis Arnold's award winning trading system chosen as "Trading Method of the Year" by Super Trader's Almanac.

☐ PPS Software - Based on Pattern Probability Strategy, this software prints all your signals and stops for the next day in less than two minutes. (Requires CSI or Technical Tools data)

☐ Money Management - Requires your phone number for personal contact.

-----------------------------------------------------------------------------

Tear out and mail to:

Curtis Arnold
5585 Center Street
Jupiter, FL 33458
or call: 407-747-1554

Name _____

Address _____

City/State/Zip _____

Phone Day _____ Evening _____

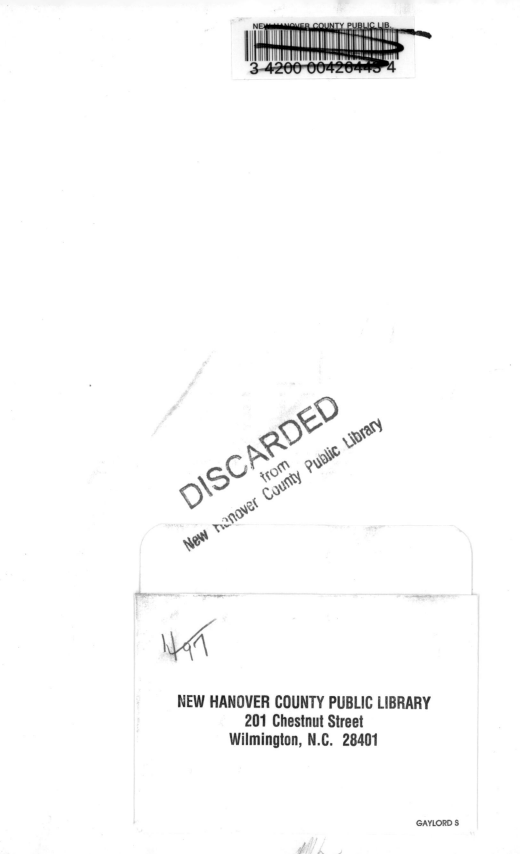

4/97

GAYLORD S